THIS MORTAL FLESH

Incarnation and Bioethics

Brent Waters

D0064570

BrazosPress

a division of Baker Publishing Group
Grand Rapids, Michigan

Published by Brazos Press
a division of Baker Publishing Group
P.O. Box 6287, Grand Rapids, MI 49516-6287
www.brazospress.com

Printed in the United States of America

Library of Congress Cataloging-in-Publication Data

Waters, Brent.
    This mortal flesh : incarnation and bioethics / Brent Waters.
        p.   cm.
    Includes bibliographical references and index.
    ISBN 978-1-58743-251-4 (pbk.)
    1. Bioethics—Religious aspects—Christianity. 2. Medical ethics—Religious aspects—Christianity. 3. Christian ethics. I. Title.
QH332.W38 2009
241′.64957—dc22   2009014707

THIS
MORTAL
FLESH

To Ronald Cole-Turner

Contents

Preface

The purpose of this book is to encourage and assist Christians to reflect on the formation, practice, and meaning of their faith in light of selected bioethical issues. In many respects, medicine or healthcare serves as a surrogate religion within late modern society. Although a concern for health is compatible with Christian belief and practice, recent and anticipated advances, for instance, in extending longevity and enhancing performance are often based on philosophical presuppositions and religious values that are inimical to core Christian convictions. Consequently, the church must have some critical awareness of these presuppositions and values to counter their corrosive influence on the formation and enactment of the Christian moral life. The critical apparatus used throughout the book is to employ and explicate the doctrine of the incarnation in examining a range of selected bioethical issues. Each chapter represents an exploration into what it means to take mortal and finite bodies seriously, since they have been affirmed, vindicated, and redeemed by God in Christ, the Word made flesh, particularly in light of current attempts to overcome the limits of finitude and mortality. In attempting to overcome these limits is medicine unwittingly initiating a new age of Manichean disdain for the body, Gnostic search for immortality, and Pelagian quest for perfection? In addressing this question, the tone of this inquiry is neither prescriptive nor imperative, but interrogative, encouraging the reader to pursue further study and reflection.

The first chapter focuses on the convergence of biotechnology, nanotechnology, robotics, and medicine in developing various physical and cognitive enhancements. These enhancements are needed to augment individual autonomy and mobility as the premier late modern values. Moreover, the underlying premise for such enhancement is that humans should use technology to make themselves better than human in order to develop and take advantage of their full potential. Although these enhancements purportedly offer longer, healthier, and happier lives, I argue that they represent an implicit loathing of the body, and, more importantly, the finitude and mortality it represents. In response, I contend that such loathing is unwarranted, for it is as mortal and finite creatures that God in Christ affirms, vindicates, and redeems human beings.

The following chapter initiates a series of investigations of specific issues that cumulatively disclose healthcare as the salvific religion of late modernity, and medicine as the principal means of achieving its proffered salvation. Chapter 2 concentrates on reproductive technology. It begins by examining the problems of infertility in the Old Testament, and contending that the problem at issue there is not identical to what is portrayed as its late modern counterpart that can be rectified through recourse to various reproductive technologies. In reaction to the claim that autonomous persons have the right to pursue their respective reproductive interests, utilizing whatever collaborative and technological assistance might be required, I argue that Christians should think about the vocation of parenthood in respect to their witness of offering hospitality to children instead of correcting the "problem" of infertility.

Chapter 3 examines recent developments in human genetics and their promising medical applications. Although these developments are admittedly beneficial, the popular perception of genes determining an individual's fate should be resisted, to avoid the prospect of genetics becoming the new astrology. In countering genetic fatalism, I examine the relation between Christ and destiny and how it might be applied to the relation between genetics and medicine.

The next chapter visits the highly controversial issue of human embryonic stem cell research and therapeutic cloning. It is argued that the current debates over the personhood of embryos are not productive, since they cannot relieve the current political gridlock over the moral status of the human embryo. As an alternative for public moral debate, I propose that embryos should be regarded as neighbors. Subsequently, I discuss selected ethical implications and suggest public policy guidelines governing research and the role Christians might play in their formulation.

Chapter 5 assesses current and anticipated developments in regenerative medicine. The principal argument is that this revolutionary movement in healthcare is premised on the portrayal of aging as a disease that can and should be treated aggressively. If aging is a disease that can be treated, however, then it can also presumably be cured, a presumption that is tantamount to waging a war against mortality. Winning this war, however, effectively requires humans to aspire to become posthuman. In response, I argue that such an endeavor is futile, since it is based on a corrupt portrayal of Christian eschatology in which immortality is achieved by rendering death mute. In contrast, Christians allow death to speak but do not grant it the final word, since they are resurrected into the eternal life of the Triune God. The following chapter builds upon this inquiry by claiming that regenerative medicine and, more broadly, the posthuman project are based on the misleading assumption that the human condition can best be relieved by using technology to transform mortal flesh into immortal data. In contrast, I contend that genuine hope is grounded in the incarnation in which the Word was made flesh.

Chapter 7 asserts that the posthuman project generally and medical attempts to radically extend longevity in particular stem from the unreasonable presupposition that death is unfair and irrational. Following Hannah Arendt, natality and mortality are the principal brackets that delineate and define the human condition. Late modernity's fixation on the latter to the detriment of the former distorts social and political ordering by asserting the tyrannical control of the present generation over both past and future counterparts. Such tyranny is in play in posthuman rhetoric in its advocacy of technologies that are designed to extend personal survival for as long as possible (perhaps forever). In contrast, Christians consent to their mortality, which enables them to be self-giving to future generations. This more just intergenerational relationship is suggested by the incarnation, death, and resurrection of Jesus Christ. The following chapter continues this inquiry by criticizing the posthuman project

11

as a combination of nihilism and Pelagianism, the will to power combined with a desire for perfection, however ill conceived such a notion might prove to be. In this respect, posthumanism is a classic example of St. Augustine's understanding of sin as disordered desire. In response, I maintain that properly ordered desire rests in aligning the human will with God's will, however imperfectly it is perceived and practiced, and that perfection lies in eternal fellowship with the Triune God as an eschatological promise that is received as a gift of grace rather than attained through the technological transformation of the human species.

The final chapter examines the ultimate late modern hope of achieving immortality by transforming human identity into data that can be stored and downloaded into robotic or virtual reality hosts. I argue that this hope stems from the prevalent, but mistaken, late modern belief that information is superior to narration, that the image has supplanted the word. This supplanting is problematic for Christian faith, since the gospel is a narration of God's judgment and grace rather than the conveyance and manipulation of divine information. Consequently, Christians need to recover the centrality of the Word, that their lives, as mortal and finite creatures, may be conformed to Christ.

The book consists of material that has been published previously and lectures delivered over the past few years. Much of the material has been substantially edited to update pertinent information and to avoid redundancies, although some key arguments or descriptions are repeated to maintain the flow of particular chapters. Chapter 1 is a highly condensed version of the Harry C. Vollmar Lectures that were delivered in Bay View, Michigan. Chapter 2 appeared originally as an article in *New Conversations* (2002), and an edited version is included with the permission of the publisher. Chapter 3 was delivered initially as a lecture at the Creative Learning Institute in Rochester, Minnesota, and a similar version was delivered at St. Andrews College, Laurinburg, North Carolina. Chapter 4 was delivered originally as a lecture at the Medical College of Wisconsin, Wauwatosa, and similar versions were delivered at International College, Naples, Florida; Grove City College, Grove City, Pennsylvania; and the De Pree Leadership Center, Pasadena, California. Chapter 5 was delivered initially as a lecture at Hong Kong Baptist University and subsequently published as an article in *The Journal of Medicine and Philosophy* 34:3 (June 2009). An edited version is included with the permission of the publisher. Some material is also adapted from my book *From Human to Posthuman*, published by Ashgate. Chapter 6 appeared originally as an article in *Christian Bioethics* 11:3 (December 2005), and an edited version is included with the permission of the publisher. Chapters 7 and 8 were delivered initially as lectures at Trinity International University, Bannockburn, Illinois, and reprinted as articles in *Ethics and Medicine* 25:1 (summer 2009) and 25:2 (fall 2009) respectively. Edited versions of these articles are included with the permission of the publisher. Chapter 9 was delivered originally as a lecture at Garrett-Evangelical Theological Seminary, Evanston, Illinois.

I am grateful to Steve Ayers at Baker Publishing Group for his initial encouragement to pursue this project, and I am indebted to Rodney Clapp, editorial director of Brazos Press, who has helped clarify the tone and scope of the book throughout its development and eventual completion. Jeremiah Gibbs, a doctoral student at Garrett-Evangelical Theological Seminary, has served ably as my research assistant, often going beyond the call of duty, and I am particularly thankful that he took on, with remarkable good humor, the odious chore of compiling the index. I am also obliged to Dean Lallene Rector and President Philip Amerson of Garrett-Evangelical Theological Seminary for granting me a sabbatical to complete the necessary writing and editing, and more broadly for their continuing support and encouragement. I have been blessed with good students and colleagues over the years who have been generous with their time in conversing with me on a number of topics addressed in this book, especially Dong Hwan Kim, Jason Gill, Sondra Wheeler, Robert Song, Ben Mitchell, Chris Hook, George Kalantzis, Steve Long, and David Hogue. I have benefited greatly from their keen observations and critical comments. As always my wife, Diana, patiently endured my preoccupation with the topic of this book, serving as a constant reminder that vulnerable and finite people are bound together through strong and enduring bonds of love. Finally, the book is dedicated to Ron Cole-Turner, to acknowledge both our long collaboration on a number of projects and publications pertaining to bioethics and, more importantly, our equally long friendship. He will no doubt quarrel with a number of claims I make in the following pages, but it is largely his work that prompts me to think about bioethics in light of core theological convictions, and I hope these essays will invite further conversations.

1

How Brave a New World?

God, Technology, and Medicine

I rarely mention bioethics in this chapter. Rather, technology is the principal focus of my inquiry and exposition. To understand the import of contemporary healthcare, the dominant formative role of technology cannot be ignored. This is the case not only because healthcare is delivered increasingly through high-tech treatments and devices, but that arguably technology is the ontology of late modernity. Consequently, bioethical issues are embedded within this ontology and cannot be separated from a late modern culture that places its hope in the technological mastery of nature and human nature. In this chapter I examine some selected aspects of this drive toward mastery and provide a critical and interpretive framework for addressing a range of bioethical topics in subsequent chapters.

What Is This New World?

In the opening paragraph of *Brave New World*, we encounter the motto of the book's fictional "World State": "COMMUNITY, IDENTITY, STABILITY."[1] Huxley describes how various technologies are used to achieve these ambitious goals. Sexual pleasure and procreation have become entirely separated. Babies are conceived and gestated artificially in hatcheries, where they are also genetically engineered and socially programmed to conform their behavior to a rigid caste system. Since the possibility of pregnancy has been removed, individuals are free to have as many sex partners as they might choose; marriage and family have been effectively abolished.

The drug *soma* is readily available and taken frequently. It amplifies pleasurable experiences and emotions while blunting their negative counterparts, thereby preventing depression and antisocial behavior. There is an abundance of leisure time to take advantage of entertaining diversions such as the "feelies," a cinematic experience that adds tactile stimulation to the film's visual and audio effects. At the end of life, hospitals offer euthanasia services that proffer a death free of pain and anxiety.

Not everyone, however, is included in this utopia. There are "savages" who have chosen not to partake of these technological blessings. They are confined to reservations so that their Luddite superstitions will not contaminate the welfare of the larger and more progressive society. They are regarded as a public nuisance and an enemy of the state who must be monitored and sequestered.

Except for the savages, the inhabitants of this brave new world are happy, healthy, and content. Their lives are largely free of physical pain and emotional stress. They are spared the expense and burden of childrearing, and face the prospect of an easy death. Yet there is a price to be paid, for it is also a world virtually devoid of passion, much less love, a world in which freedom has been debased to little more than self-indulgence. More troubling still is that Huxley's fictional world is not all that different from our own late modern world.

Brave New World is a remarkable book, given that it was written in 1932. The point is not to assess Huxley's predictive abilities. Many of his predictions were simply wrong. Babies, for example, are not born in hatcheries. What Huxley perceived correctly was that the approaching development of biomedical technologies would have a profound influence in shaping social institutions and political structures. When sexual pleasure is separated from procreation, there is little need for marriage and family. The desire to avoid pain and suffering makes euthanasia an attractive option. Physical and mental health can be improved with drugs and other medical interventions.

What Huxley perceived with great clarity is that technology forms the patterns of daily life, as well as the values and convictions of the people who live out their lives within these patterns. Technology requires that the meanings of community, identity, and stability are defined in a particular way. To think about technology is to ponder the question of our very being as late moderns: who are we, and what are we aspiring to become? Consequently, Huxley's book may serve as a mirror that both clarifies and distorts these questions.

A similar sentiment is captured in George Grant's adage, "In each lived moment of our waking and sleeping, we are technological civilisation."[2] What Grant means is something more than the fact that late moderns spend a great deal of their time in the company of machines and gadgets. It is difficult, if not impossible, to imagine what it would be like to live in world devoid of any objects crafted by human beings. We cannot define who we are or express what we aspire to become in the absence of technology. The question posed by Grant, however, is, What are the underlying values and convictions that are operative in placing our confidence in technologies that purportedly enable us to live better lives?

To answer that question we must first turn our attention to that troubled philosopher, Friedrich Nietzsche. According to Grant, "There is no escape from reading Nietzsche if one would understand modernity."[3] His "words raise to an intensely full light of explicitness what it is to live in this era."[4] He is, as characterized by Joan O'Donovan, the premier seer and conscience of the late modern world.[5] There are many aspects of his thinking that warrant examination, but a brief summary of his idea of the "historical sense" will suffice.

Nietzsche's chief complaint with his fellow philosophers is that they waste their time contemplating an eternal Good that simply does not exist, but is a fantasy projected upon an indifferent world. All we have is a history we have constructed, and a future that we think we want to construct. Human beings—both individually and collectively—are little more than bundles of either aggressive or passive wills. It is this will to power, rather than any moral or spiritual notions of the Good, that defines who we are and what we aspire

17

to become. And as Nietzsche's astute interpreter Martin Heidegger has observed, it is through technology that the will to power is effectively asserted.[6] To return to the motto of Huxley's brave new world, we construct our *communities* and *identities,* and it is the sheer power of our will and what we will that provide the *stability* for undertaking these construction projects.

Community

The will to power is asserted first and foremost in the attempt to master nature. Natural resources are extracted from the earth and transformed into energy or artifacts. Cities increasingly dominate the global landscape and are connected by elaborate transportation infrastructures and communication networks. The "natural" habitat of late moderns is largely one of their own fabrication. Their corporate identity is that of *homo faber*—the creatures who construct a reality that they will into being through the power of their technology.

In constructing our communities the constraints of time and place are increasingly eased and ignored. Many communities are now comprised of people who are not in close geographic proximity to one another. The communities that we find most meaningful are not necessarily the ones we were born into, but those we choose to join or help create. We are born, for instance, in specific towns and countries, but that does not preclude the possibility of frequently relocating or emigrating.

Yet nowhere is the growing irrelevancy of time and place more apparent than in the changing patterns of how and when we work, and the widening gap between where we work and where we reside. Quite a bit can be accomplished without having any face-to-face contact with another person, at a time and location of our choosing. Imagine, for example, that I need a new laptop computer. While on a trip in a hotel room late at night I order a computer online and request delivery on the day I will return home. In the few minutes that it took me to complete this task, I initiated a series of global transactions. Although the headquarters of the company from which I purchased the computer is located in Texas, the server hosting the Web site is in Vancouver. An office worker in Dublin reviews and processes my order. The hardware and software were manufactured in such places as Bucharest, Seoul, and Taipei. My computer is assembled in Shanghai and air-freighted and delivered to my door at the appointed time by a corporation headquartered in Memphis.

There are admittedly limits to the extent that technology can change how and when work is performed. If a water pipe breaks in my house, it will do me no good to call a plumber in Warsaw; I need one close by who can arrive in a timely manner. Although time and place are not entirely irrelevant, they are less pertinent in constructing relationships and communities. Information and transportation technologies in particular allow late moderns to overcome many of the constraints of time and place that their ancestors took for granted. The difference between what is local and what is global grows less defined with each passing year. Consequently, it is presumed that many, if not most, of our communities should be comprised of individuals sharing common interests rather than thrown together accidentally or haphazardly. Moreover, since one's interests change over time, it is also assumed that communities should also change in a corresponding manner; a community can be as easily torn down as constructed. Arguably, late modern communities are comprised of high-tech nomads.

Identity

To move on to the second word in the motto of Huxley's new world, what does it mean to have a nomadic *identity*? High-tech nomads must be both mobile and autonomous. Such mobility is not limited to the ability to move about physically but includes, more importantly, what may be described as an imaginative and social mobility. This mobility is useful in constructing unique—to use that peculiar term beloved by Nietzsche's disciples—lifestyles. Late moderns can imagine a far greater range of lifestyle possibilities than previous generations envisioned, and, unlike their ancestors, they can actualize many of these possibilities so long as adequate financial resources and access to requisite services are available. The value of mobility is particularly pronounced in a globally integrated economy in which a premium is placed on the rapid and efficient exchange of information. The mobile communication device is the symbol of power in the late modern world, because it can be used virtually anytime and anyplace. So long as one is connected, it does not matter where one lives and where one works; the distance between workplace and residence is rendered insignificant. In addition, mobile people must be autonomous individuals. Taking full advantage of one's mobility requires independence from the constraints of physical, social, and emotional attachments. As befits a nomadic lifestyle, late moderns are always on the move, frequently changing jobs, careers, houses, hobbies, colleagues, friends, and even spouses.

Most importantly, mobile and autonomous people must also be physically healthy and mentally alert. Ill health or mental deterioration makes a person more dependent upon others, and dependency impinges upon mobility and autonomy. Consequently, late moderns turn to medicine to protect these cherished values. If technology in general enables the construction of communities of mobile and autonomous individuals, and medicine in turn promotes greater autonomy and mobility, then we encounter an intriguing dilemma: how is the proffered *stability* of Huxley's brave new world achieved? If people are genuinely free, then will they not inevitably pursue interests that in some, if not many, instances may be in conflict? This situation seems to create a chaotic rather than a stable situation, yet it is precisely this chaos that is the prerequisite for the putative stability of the late modern world.

What Is Brave about This New World?

There is a scene in *Brave New World* in which the Controller is addressing a crowd: " 'Stability,' " said the Controller, " 'stability. No civilization without social stability. No social stability without individual stability.' His voice was a trumpet. Listening they felt larger, warmer." Later he reiterates: " 'Stability,' insisted the Controller, 'stability. The primal and ultimate need. Stability.' "[7] What should be highlighted in this exuberant oratory is the intrinsic and mutually reinforcing relationship between the collective and the personal. A stable society is based on stable individuals, and stable individuals are developed within stable communities. Hence the need to control reproduction through a combination of artificial wombs and genetic engineering, and the need to control behavior through indoctrination and extensive use of drugs such as *soma*.

According to Huxley, social and individual stability can be achieved only through centralized planning of the ubiquitous "World State." Ironically, the political foundation of this brave new world is based on the organizational principles of Henry Ford. Throughout the book Ford is invoked as a messianic figure, and Fordism functions as a de facto religion. This scion of capitalism becomes the inspiration for a social and political order based on centralized planning and totalitarian control. The prospect is not as far-fetched as it might appear to be, for the early leaders of the Soviet Union were rather taken with Mr. Ford and applied his organizational principles in developing their industrial policies. The Soviets assumed that when combined with more "efficient" centralized planning, proletarian workers would be more productive than their capitalist counterparts. Moreover, we must again recall the circumstances surrounding the 1932 publication date of Huxley's masterpiece. With the world mired in the Great Depression, capitalism had apparently run its course and was headed toward extinction.

It is this prospect of a world state that represents Huxley's greatest failure as a prognosticator. He is not to be faulted, however, because he failed to foresee the eventual collapse of the Soviet Union. Huxley's failure is not his inaccurate prediction, but that he failed to recognize that the stability his brave new world required could not be achieved by any global government. A stable world of autonomous and mobile individuals requires radical decentralization. Stability is largely, though not entirely, the result of interactions and exchanges that are free and unplanned, whereas instability is the consequence of tightly controlled planning and administration. A stable society is one in which no one seems to be in charge.

Control, no control, and the mastery of nature

This admittedly counterintuitive claim is Paul Seabright's chief argument in his book *The Company of Strangers: A Natural History of Economic Life*.[8] Globalization works, for instance, because no individual, committee, or government is in the position to determine what goods and services should be produced, and how they are manufactured, distributed, and purchased. Rather, various individuals perform discrete and specialized tasks in response to the demands of global markets. Seabright calls this "tunnel vision," and it is the sum total of narrow tunnels that result in more expansive and relatively stable channels of economic exchange. To return to the example of my purchasing a new computer, a worker in a microchip factory in Taipei does not start her day by thinking that she is making some chips for Mr. Waters in America, or that her work is contributing to the greater glory of Taiwan. She is instead fixated on the narrow task of constructing microchips, and she is compelled to do her work by the prospect that producing defective ones could mean losing her job to more motivated competitors in Shanghai. It is through the collective efforts of sales representatives, accountants, microchip manufacturers, assemblers, and freight deliverers that my new computer is delivered to my door. Remarkably, no one is in charge of the overall process.

The idea that efficient economic exchange thrives in the absence of centralized planning and control seemingly defies common sense. It is generally assumed that when no one is in charge, chaos results. Seabright became aware of this intuition while advising bakers of an Eastern European city on how to adapt to market mechanisms following the fall of communism. He described elaborate mechanisms for producing, distributing, and consuming bread in London, which is highly efficient given the large number of small, independent bakers, distributors, and shops. An equilibrium is established between supply and demand in which there is little wastage, and almost never any shortages; Londoners have little difficulty in obtaining their daily bread. His clients were impressed but also bewildered, for they asked, But who is in charge of deciding how much bread to bake and where it should be sold? He had great difficulty explaining that the system worked efficiently because no single agent or agency was in a position to make those decisions.

The key factor underlying free yet orderly exchanges is that humans routinely trust and cooperate with strangers, and more often than not these qualities are learned and reinforced through informal interactions. Pandemonium is avoided because these interactions carry with them equally informal, yet highly effective, rewards and punishments. If I discover that a colleague is a hopeless gossip, for

22

instance, I will not entrust him with secrets. More expansively, I do not obtain my new computer because an agency of the United Nations regulates each aspect of its design, production, and distribution. Rather, I trust that a sales representative will process my order instead of tossing it in the bin; that good rather than defective chips are installed; and that the deliverer will ring my doorbell and tell me to have a nice day instead of beating me up and robbing me. These trustworthy and cooperative interactions are rewarded by customers purchasing the products of reliable companies and suppliers.

The ability to trust and cooperate with strangers is a rare phenomenon. Human beings are evidently the only species that has developed this capacity. It is noteworthy because it seemingly runs counter to the nature that evolution has bequeathed to humans. It is not natural to trust or cooperate with strangers, and there are good evolutionary reasons why this is so. Our distant ancestors were hunters and gatherers. Beyond a narrow range of kinship, there were strong incentives to be wary of other humans. When one's kinship group is competing with other groups for scarce supplies of food, a rational strategy is to avoid, chase away, or kill strangers. Yet humans now interact with apparent comfort and ease with a host of strangers on a daily basis; what is seemingly contrary to their nature has become their second nature. In Seabright's evocative words: "Within a few hundred generations—barely a pause for breath in evolutionary time—[humans] had formed social organizations of startling complexity. Not just village settlements but cities, armies, empires, corporations, nation states, political movements, humanitarian organizations, even internet communities. The same shy, murderous ape that had avoided strangers throughout its evolutionary history was now living, working, and moving among complete strangers in their millions."[9]

Although humans carry the "murderous ape" in their genes, they have, to a large extent, learned to control it. They do not routinely avoid, chase away, or kill strangers. Indeed, as inhabitants of the late modern world they must trust and cooperate with strangers to conduct their daily affairs. How has this come to be? We may say that biological evolution is being increasingly displaced by what may be characterized as "cultural evolution" as the dominant, formative feature of human life. To paraphrase Grant, late moderns are forming a culture predicated upon the progressive mastery of nature and human nature. To survive and thrive as a species, and as individuals, they must simultaneously reshape the natural, social, and political environments in which they live, while also transforming themselves within those environments. What is "brave" about this new world is not the belief that nature and human nature should be mastered, but that humans are developing the technology to complete this twofold task in an efficient and comprehensive manner.

As was mentioned in the preceding section, humans are becoming increasingly adept at mastering nature. They reshape the landscape with their cities, with plants and animals that are genetically altered to increase agricultural productivity, and easing the constraints of time and place through instant communication and rapid transportation. Late moderns have come to perceive nature largely as a collection of resources at their disposal in enabling their mobility and enhancing their autonomy. As technological development becomes more extensive, a world of ubiquitous machines, gadgets, and devices becomes their "natural" habitat; late moderns are most at home in a world they have fabricated for themselves. Moreover, the growing formative influence of technology takes on an aura of inevitability, for humans grow steadily more dependent upon the instruments they employ in their mastery of nature.

This mounting mastery of nature, however, raises an important issue: how do late moderns master human nature so that they may live more peaceably and productively in a world of their own making, but a world in which biological evolution has not prepared them to live? The murderous ape has been tamed but is not extinct. Humans must transform themselves into beings that are formed by their cultural evolution; they must become more fully the product of their own purposeful will than outcomes of natural selection. Consequently, the goal is to maximize self-determination, for in a world of mobile and autonomous individuals in which stability is achieved through the absence of overt control, stable individuals are required to maintain a stable social order. This task is undertaken primarily through enculturation, but despite the progressive mastery of human nature stubborn natural and biological limits remain.

Medicine and the mastery of human nature

Medicine is used as the principal tool in overcoming these limits that prevent a more extensive, and presumably desirable, transformation of individual human beings. Specifically, a threefold strategy of therapy, prevention, and enhancement is employed. Improved therapies are being developed to restore mobility and protect autonomy in response to illness, injury, and aging. Great advances are being made, for instance, in developing drugs, implants, and surgical techniques to repair clogged arteries and damaged hearts. Sophisticated prosthetics are available and constantly being improved to compensate for lost or damaged limbs. Monitoring and communication devices are helping elderly people overcome short-term memory loss and remain independent. Improved testing and screening techniques are being developed and employed to prevent fatal or debilitating illnesses. Tests designed to detect the early onset of arterial or coronary disease are readily employed, as are subsequent drug regimes to prevent or retard further development. In addition, screening embryos and fetuses to detect, and prevent the birth of children with, various genetically related diseases and disabilities, such as cystic fibrosis or Down syndrome, is becoming a standard practice in prenatal care. Moreover, it is anticipated that new techniques for improving physical and mental performance are imminent. These include drugs to enhance cardiovascular functions, physical strength, mental concentration, and memory recall, as well as artificial organs, veins, and brain implants.

The application of these therapeutic, preventive, and enhancement technologies is part of the larger task of blurring the line separating the natural and the artificial. Mastering nature requires the creation of a hybrid culture, one that is neither natural nor artificial, for late moderns perceive nature through the lens of their technological manipulation. Urbanites and suburbanites encounter "nature" in well-manicured parks and yards, and if they undertake an adventurous diversion in a protected wilderness, they do so with the best available clothing, equipment, navigational aids, and communication devices.

The closely related task of mastering human nature also requires blurring the line separating the natural and the artificial. A culture predicated upon mobility and autonomy must be populated by mobile and autonomous individuals. High-tech nomads literally embody their technology. They eat genetically modified plants and animals, take medicines derived from the latest advances in chemical engineering and biotechnology, and carry surgically implanted stents, pacemakers, and plastic joints; and prolonged contact with information and communication technologies physically forms their brains. Late moderns are both the beneficiaries *and* the artifacts of their technology, and as such they represent a future that is both promising and perilous.

The plight of Matt Nagle may serve to illustrate this promise and peril.[10] At the age of twenty he was stabbed during a brawl, and since then has been paralyzed from the neck down, unable to use his arms or legs. Yet Matt can turn the lights on and off in his room, change the channels and adjust the volume on the television, and receive and send e-mail through the power of his mind. With the aid of an electrode implanted in his brain, he thinks "turn the light on," "raise the volume," and "move the cursor and click," and with voice recognition software writes a message. The light, television, and computer obey his commands. It is hoped that this new technology of cyberkinetics may also one day enable him to bypass his injury by using his mind to order his legs to walk, and his arms and hands to move.

Although this technology is in its infancy, it is nonetheless an astonishing achievement and holds great promise for individuals suffering paralysis and amputation. It is anticipated that this same technology could also be used to control artificial limbs as well as paralyzed ones. Perhaps someday this technology will not only provide patients with virtual mobility and autonomy (e.g., using a computer), but also restore physical mobility and personal independence. Moreover, as this technology grows more sophisticated, it can be adapted to help anyone control a computer, mobile phone, and other devices. Admittedly, electrodes implanted in the brain are uncomfortable and run the risk of infection, so alternatively a cap with sensors fitted snugly on the head is being developed. With the help of this device, individuals have been able to control computer keyboards and play computer games solely through the power of their minds.

Therapeutic applications of cyberkinetics are welcomed achievements, but like most technologies also have sinister potential. The same technology that is used to control objects can also be deployed to control behavior. Researchers have implanted electrodes in the brains of rats and guided their movement through a maze with a joystick. The same device that enables a person to manipulate objects also exposes her to the possibility of being manipulated. More broadly, late moderns face the prospect that their technological capability may move beyond their biological ability to keep pace. Some computer scientists anticipate, for example, that around 2020 or 2030 the computational speed of computers will exceed the ability of the human brain to use them properly. Consequently, the brain will need to be enhanced if humans are to take full advantage of information technology. More expansively, there is the problem of aging to be overcome. Unfortunately, humans do not live long enough to fully maximize their potential. They need to transform themselves as individuals and as a species so that they can live longer without the loss of physical strength, youthful vigor, and mental agility. To live well in the world that humans are creating for themselves, they also need to transform themselves into something better than human, a superior posthuman being.

It is this prospect of radical transformation combined with the potentially sinister side of technological development that leads back to the stability of Huxley's brave new world. For this world requires both stable individuals and a stable society, requiring control techniques more subtle than Huxley envisioned, and more extensive in their transformative power than he imagined. What is brave about this new world is the audacity of humans taking their fate into their own hands; of using their technological power to recreate themselves in their own image. But this prospect raises some intriguing questions: What is this image? Is it an image that should be endorsed? Or more pointedly, is this brave new world a good world?

Is This New World a Good World?

Toward the end of Huxley's book, the brave new world is defended by one of its prominent leaders in an argument with the Savage. The leader asserts that " 'industrial civilization is only possible when there's no self-denial. Self-indulgence up to the very limits imposed by hygiene and economics. Otherwise the wheels stop turning.' " He adds that passion must be controlled, because it threatens the stability of the social order. " 'And instability means the end of civilization. You can't have a lasting civilization without plenty of pleasant vices.' "[11]

In a rambling speech the leader spells out the benefits of these plentiful vices, insisting that

> civilization has absolutely no need of nobility or heroism. These things are symptoms of political inefficiency. In a properly organized society like ours, nobody has any opportunities for being noble or heroic. Conditions have got to be thoroughly unstable before the occasion can arise. Where there are . . . divided allegiances, where there are temptations to be resisted, objects of love to be fought for or defended—there, obviously, nobility and heroism have some sense. . . . The greatest care is taken to prevent you from loving any one too much. There's no such thing as a divided allegiance; you're so conditioned that you can't help doing what you ought to do. And what you ought to do is on the whole so pleasant . . . that there really aren't any temptations to resist. And if ever, by some unlucky chance, anything unpleasant should somehow happen, why, there's always *soma* to give you a holiday from the facts. And there's always *soma* to calm your anger, to reconcile you to your enemies, to make you patient and long-suffering. In the past you could only accomplish these things by making a great effort and after years of hard moral training. Now you swallow two or three half-gramme tablets, and there you are. Anybody can be virtuous now. . . . Christianity without tears—that's what *soma* is.[12]

This leader of the brave new world is offering a life free of pain and suffering; a world where the unpleasant necessity of moral constraint and self-denial is not needed. As was noted above, this new world is created through the mastery of nature and human nature, and two misgivings were also suggested regarding this project. First, technologies that are used to improve the quality of life can also be employed to manipulate behavior. The same apparatus enabling a paralyzed patient to open e-mail could also be deployed to turn

28

a person into the equivalent of a rat in a maze. Second, to keep pace with anticipated technological developments that maximize the potential of mobile and autonomous individuals, humans will need to transform themselves into a better species. Creating stable individuals and a stable social order requires posthuman transformation. How might this leader of the brave new world respond to these misgivings?

In response to the fear that technology can be used to manipulate behavior, he might reply, "So what?" Individuals are already manipulated by others in countless and subtle ways. An individual's behavior is influenced by various relationships, social settings, and political institutions. What is being proffered is simply a more efficient and beneficial way of being manipulated. The leader may concede that a magic pill such as *soma* is probably not forthcoming, but there are other promising medicinal solutions for helping individuals deal with unfortunate events. They can be provided a "holiday from the facts," their anxieties relieved and their grieving soothed. In addition, their pleasure can be amplified. Why, for instance, should anyone hesitate to pop some pills that enhance one's concentration and diminish one's need for sleep? Most importantly, why object to using drugs or other therapies that would help a person to ignore—or better, forget—the naked facts of what is at times a harsh and cruel world? Recent advances in the neurosciences regarding short-term memory, for example, hold promising therapeutic applications. In a trial run, women treated in an emergency ward following a rape or an assault were given medication that reduced their recall of the traumatic event. Such intervention is credited with helping some of these women to cope better, avoiding many of the psychological ill effects, such as depression or paralyzing fear. The ultimate goal is to eventually remove any memory of tragic events altogether. More speculatively, selected long-term memories might also be eliminated, easing the plight of adults who are suffering the psychological effects of abuse or neglect as children.

It may be objected that this is a dishonest strategy, because it is based on a sanitized and partial reality, to which the leader might reply, "Why assume that what is remembered is real?" No one has total or accurate recall. Memories are highly subjective, interpretive, and selective. Indeed, no one could survive the crushing weight of naked and uninterpreted remembering. What these treatments provide is more efficient and effective control in improving the psychological health of individuals and thereby social stability. People liberated from unpleasant memories are happy persons. Happy persons produce stable individuals. Stable individuals preserve a stable social order. Why should individuals be condemned to suffer the ill effects of traumatic or unpleasant memories when the power to remove them is available? Why refrain from memory control in a new world whose stability is predicated upon and dedicated to enabling unfettered self-indulgence? What is wrong, in short, with Christianity without tears?

The leader's reply to the second misgiving might entail the insistence that if we are concerned about the sinister side of technological manipulation, then we should also have no qualms about the prospect of posthuman transformation. If the issue is remembering a so-called reality, then humans need to refashion themselves as beings with the requisite power to construct so-called real experiences that provide pleasant memories. There is nothing wrong with humans transforming themselves into superior beings, for do they want to trust their fate to natural processes which are, at best, indifferent if not inimical to their flourishing? Is not the purposeful control of human life afforded by technological manipulation preferable to the chance and necessity of natural selection? Moreover, by enhancing physical and mental capabilities, is not the supreme value of freedom fully embraced and effectually enacted? For there can be no greater freedom than having the power to transform oneself into becoming the kind of person he or she desires to be. In a world relatively free of pain, suffering, and hardship, of lives liberated from failed dreams and frustrated ambition, late moderns will have the opportunity to develop their full potential as mobile and autonomous individuals. With the final mastery of nature and human nature, humans take their destiny into their own hands, for the resulting new world and its inhabitants are artifacts of what they will themselves to be and to become.

Note, however, that the leader never claims that his brave new world is necessarily a good world. Nor can he make such a claim, for the freedom he offers requires a world that is beyond good and evil. Even these basic moral categories impose intolerable constraints upon freedom, namely, the freedom of an unconstrained will to become what it wants to be. What he offers is a world in which its inhabitants are free to fulfill their hearts' desires; a world that indulges alluring vices rather than practicing difficult virtues. Yet the question of whether or not such a world is good cannot be so easily dismissed or ignored. In thinking about this question we should keep in mind the Spanish proverb, "Take what you want, said God—take it and pay for it."[13] This does not suggest a simple cost–benefit analysis to calculate whether the latter outweighs the former. Rather, it acknowledges that there are no free benefits; whatever is taken entails an unavoidable cost. In their attempt to master nature and human nature, late moderns have taken greater mobility and autonomy, and are grasping for more. They have taken improved healthcare and greater longevity, and are grasping for more. They have taken enhanced physical and mental capabilities, and are grasping for more. There are admittedly many benefits that accompany this taking, but at what cost, and what is the price of grasping for more? Examining three instances will suffice to demonstrate that the price has been, and will continue to be, steep.

The costs of enhancement

The first cost is a *loathing of the body*. This is an admittedly odd claim to make in an era in which we appear to be fascinated with our bodies, and the bodies of others. A great deal of time is spent sculpting, pampering, and beautifying one's body, and considerable time and money is also spent admiring those who have done a good job of sculpting, pampering, and beautifying their bodies. We are presumably quite comfortable with our bodies, at times displaying an attitude approaching adoration. The opposite, however, is really the case. A glimpse of this deceit is captured in the leader's insistence that the brave new world should be free of any self-denial. Unfortunately, the body denies one a great deal. As embodied creatures humans are inherently fragile and vulnerable; they can be injured or become sick, they grow old and die. Because of this fragility and vulnerability, they are limited and highly dependent creatures. In a culture that values mobility and autonomy, the thought of losing one's independence and depending on others is a dreadful prospect. Consequently, late moderns work hard to preserve their health, strength, and youthful vigor so that they can stay mobile and autonomous for as long as possible. Hence, the headlong rush to develop medicines and technologies that preserve the appearance of a cherished independence.

Yet it is their fragility and vulnerability, as well as the interdependence accompanying these qualities, that make humans genuinely human. In their absence humans would be unable to learn the trust that makes their enriched social life possible. Or in theological terms, it is as embodied creatures that they bear the *imago Dei*—the image of their triune creator. Early Christian teaching insisted that the body should be neither denigrated nor indulged. The body should be disciplined by subjecting it to self-denying practices such as fasting and continence, but physical punishment should not be brutal. This is why the church has always condemned self-mutilation and torture. Moreover, doctrines claiming that the body is little more than a shell imprisoning the soul were condemned as heresies. In the evocative words of Beth Felker Jones, "in the Christian tradition, the temptation to denigrate the body has been continually reasserted and consistently rejected."[14] Contrary to the posthuman dream, hope does not reside in transforming flesh into data, but in the Word made flesh. Any new world that despises the inherently finite, fragile, and vulnerable character of being an embodied creature because of the severe constraints it places upon self-indulgence cannot be called a good world.

These conflicting hopes lead to the second cost: a *corruption of desire*. The leader insists that nobility and heroism have no roles to play in his brave new world, for the sacrifice they entail prevents self-indulgence. Heroes put the desires of others before their own, but in his new world, such self-denial is an indication of social instability rather than stability; it is the self-indulgent consumer and celebrity rather than the self-denying hero who is honored. Other people are needed only to the extent that they help one obtain what is desired. Consequently, it does not matter what is desired or how one desires, so long as no one is harmed in indulging oneself. For instance, it is not anyone else's business that I want a new computer, and I do not harm the individuals that help me obtain it.

The "what" and "how" of desire, however, *does* matter, for people become and disclose who they are through what they desire. The reasons why people want to obtain computers and the ways in which they are used are highly variable. There is a profound difference between using a computer to write articles and using it to access pornography, and these uses both shape and disclose the desires of the respective users. The issue at stake is not technology per se, for a computer does not inevitably force one to adopt evil or wicked desires; rather, it can easily corrupt the desire for what are often good things.[15] There is nothing intrinsically wrong in wanting to write articles or in sexual longing, but these healthy desires are distorted if the Internet is used to plagiarize or indulge fantasies that separate sex from intimacy. One of the great insights of St. Augustine was that sin was not so much the result of desiring bad things, but of desiring good things badly. As he observed in the *City of God*, there was nothing wrong with Rome's desire for social and political order. The problem was that Rome loved the glory of conquest more than it did justice, thereby corrupting that good desire.[16]

The proper ordering of desire is one of the most pressing issues faced by contemporary Christians. Mobility and autonomy, for example, are goods to be desired, but not at the price of denigrating the goods of fellowship and locality. Individual identity can develop properly only by belonging with others, and mutual belonging requires a given place in which to flourish.[17] There is nothing wrong in desiring good health, but not when it becomes a consuming obsession that transforms a means into an end. One properly desires good health because it enables a person to better serve and contribute to the well-being of others with whom she or he belongs. If good health becomes an end in its own right, it serves to isolate individuals from one another through an obsessive distaste for insalubrious environments, fear of contagion, or competition for access to scarce medical treatments. It is good to desire a long and productive life, but not at the expense of jeopardizing the welfare of future generations. If, however, the goal of living for as long as possible becomes predominant, then offspring are effectively reduced to liabilities, since they will consume and compete for material and financial resources needed to sustain an aging population, or worse, they will be indentured through taxation and their productivity to serve the needs of their progenitors. Any world that refuses to claim that there are certain goods that should be desired, and that there are noble and heroic ways for properly ordering their desire, cannot be called good.

What is desired ultimately shapes and discloses what is loved, which leads to the third cost: an *absence of genuine love*. This is where the leader's comments are most telling: "The greatest care is taken to prevent you from loving any one too much." Is this not the perfect ethic for a nomadic culture? No lasting allegiances or binding commitments to tie one down; no place in which to belong; no compelling necessity to invest oneself in subsequent generations. In the absence of love, one purportedly becomes impervious and invulnerable, for one cannot be severely disappointed or hurt too badly by anyone, because there simply isn't any expectation of enduring trust and fidelity. Yet to deny love—and the potential disappointment and pain it necessarily entails—is also to deny the humanity of being human creatures, for it is love that creates, sustains, and redeems them. To eliminate love is not to master human nature, but to annihilate it. Most importantly, if love is to have any substantive content, then people have a claim upon one another—a mutual belonging that both delimits and enables them to pursue the goods leading to their individual and corporate flourishing.

The ordering of love

Moreover, love is not an abstract ideal, but a quality of life that is enacted in concrete relationships and deeds. Particular kinds of people love other particular kinds of people, and love them in different and appropriate ways. Contrary to what the leader asserts, to be human necessarily entails having divided loyalties and allegiances, hence the necessity of ordering our lives within the proper priority of our loves. There is, for instance, the love of neighbors, friends, and God (or too often the gods endemic to late modernity).[18] Each of these instances requires differing and fitting expressions of love. In conducting their daily affairs, humans encounter a wide variety of neighbors. Following Karl Barth,[19] there are neighbors who are friends and those who are strangers; fellow citizens and enemies; nearby and faraway neighbors; those who are healthy and those who are sick and dying. In each case there is a concrete yet differing enactment of love: a friend may be treated with jocular familiarity while a stranger is extended courtesy and hospitality. A fellow citizen is defended from an assault by an enemy. Financial transactions bind nearby and faraway neighbors together in a global marketplace. The healthy keep company with the sick and dying. These duties and responsibilities, however, are also necessarily limited: a stranger cannot be forced to accept an offer of hospitality. Defending fellow citizens does not authorize the obliteration of all enemies. Entering the global market is not a license to commit fraud. The healthy are not entitled to end the suffering of the sick and dying by bringing their lives to an end.

In God, both the origin and end of love are encountered, so it may be said in turn that it is God who commands and empowers humans to love one another as they should be loved. They are commanded to love neighbors, be they strangers in need, friends in peril, or enemies to be resisted. They are commanded to love their families, but not to the exclusion of neighbors. They are commanded to love God with all of their heart, soul, and mind.[20] Responding to these commands may require one to foreswear or realign one's own desires in order to enact a love that is required by the origin and end of love. Contrary to the dictate of the leader, there are higher goods than self-indulgence, and love provides mutual belonging as a firmer foundation for social stability than does a collection of pleasant vices.

In addition to ordering the various loves in their particularly proper ways, there is also the task of properly ordering the hierarchy of love. What is the greatest love against which all lesser loves are ordered? The Christian answer is, of course, God. St. Ambrose once observed that "we love life as the gift of God, we love our country and our parents; lastly we love our companions with whom we like to associate. Hence arises true love, which prefers others to self, and seeks not its own . . ."[21] One may quarrel on whether or not the list is comprehensive enough, and with the ordering of the subordinate loves, but it nonetheless discloses two important tasks that are entailed in the ordering of love.

First, emphasis is placed upon the *other* rather than the self. This stress should not be interpreted as a call to denigrate oneself by always sacrificing one's self-interest for the sake of others. It is instead a tacit recognition that the self cannot be adequately formed and expressed in the absence of others. In a relationship in which all the parties are oriented toward each other, there is a mutual giving and receiving that forms the parties respectively as individuals. Ironically, in placing the self at the apex of their loves, late moderns cannot achieve the autonomy and mobility that they desire.

This priority of the self leads to the second task in the ordering of love: avoiding *idolatry*. In its most basic form, idolatry consists of placing one's ultimate love and faith upon an unwarranted person, object, or ideal. When the self is loved more than God, the resulting self-constructed self is little more than a predacious consumer of products, services, and experiences, effectively reducing others to resources to be exploited in constructing oneself. Strangers, for instance, are reduced to being workers that enable me to obtain a computer, a friend is merely a source of amusement, or my daughter is an artifact of my will. Such predatory consumption is exacerbated by the late modern confidence placed in technology as the premier instrument in constructing and fulfilling the desires of the self-made self. Hence, the fascination with and hope placed upon medicine to preserve a cosmetic youthful appearance, prevent and cure disease, enhance physical and cognitive performance, and extend longevity.

Christians must object to placing the self as the ultimate object of love, because it cannot satisfy what humans should desire, namely, fellowship with the Triune God. Such fellowship can be achieved only at God's gracious initiative, and self-made selves, regardless of how proficient their technology in general, and medicine in particular, may be, can never save themselves. Consequently, it is only by placing God at the apex of love that humankind's true desire can be fulfilled, thereby requiring the aligning of all lesser loves and desires accordingly. Contrary to the leader of the brave new world, we are necessarily a people of divided loyalties, because the singular love of God requires the delimitation and definition of the "what" and "how" of desiring. In loving God we must also love various neighbors that place disparate demands upon our time and attention. This is admittedly a daunting challenge, one the brave new world of late modernity tries to ignore by creating loveless relationships; a world devoid of love in order to eliminate the necessity of making hard choices in the ordering of our desires. There is no need to worry about what a family might require, for marriage and parenthood have been eliminated, and no need to discern and respond to the varying needs of strangers, friends, and enemies, for they have been replaced by casual and expedient acquaintances. The bonds of human affection are effectively broken or trivialized beyond recognition, and there is certainly no need to worry about God, for God has been replaced by the idol of the self. The great commandment[22] is transfigured into a tautological imperative: you shall love the self with all your heart, soul, and mind, and you shall love yourself as yourself.

To fulfill this imperative, the self must be free to construct itself, and such freedom is achieved by eliminating, through the mastery of nature and human nature, external constraints against the will. This is a false promise, however, for, again following Barth,[23] eliminating such constraints does not liberate but enslaves. It is only in the limits imposed by love that humans are free to obey God's commands so that they might become the kind of creatures God created them to be. It is only within the finite and temporal limits of a created order that humans are freed for fellowship with God. Consequently, Christians must resist the idolatrous faith in technology and medicine if they are to embrace the freedom offered by God, a task requiring courage.

How Can We Be Genuinely Brave in a Brave New World?

Toward the end of Huxley's *Brave New World,* there is a revealing exchange between the Controller and the Savage. The Savage asks,

> "Isn't there something in living dangerously?"
>
> "There's a great deal in it," the Controller replied. "Men and women must have their adrenals stimulated from time to time."
>
> "What?" questioned the Savage, uncomprehending.
>
> "It's one of the conditions of perfect health. That's why we've made the V.P.S. treatments compulsory."
>
> "V.P.S.?"
>
> "Violent Passion Surrogate. Regularly once a month. We flood the whole system with adrenin. It's the complete physiological equivalent of fear and rage. All the tonic effects of murdering Desdemona and being murdered by Othello, without any of the inconveniences."

"But I like the inconveniences."

"We don't," said the Controller. "We prefer to do things comfortably."

"But I don't want comfort. I want God, I want poetry, I want real danger, I want freedom, I want goodness. I want sin."

"In fact," said [the Controller], "you're claiming the right to be unhappy."

"All right then," said the Savage defiantly, "I'm claiming the right to be unhappy."

"Not to mention the right to grow old and ugly and impotent; the right to have syphilis and cancer; the right to have too little to eat; the right to be lousy; the right to live in constant apprehension of what may happen to-morrow; the right to catch typhoid; the right to be tortured by unspeakable pains of every kind." There was a long silence.

"I claim them all," said the Savage at last.[24]

This conversation captures the essence of Huxley's masterpiece, for the reader confronts two stark and diametrically opposed options regarding the future. The Controller offers a world free of pain, suffering, and discomfort, but devoid of passion, while the Savage contends that it is precisely discomfort, suffering, and pain that give life meaning. The former plays it safe, while the latter lives dangerously. The Controller insists that if humans are to flourish, they must master nature and human nature, while the Savage counters that if humans are to remain human, they must conform their lives to their true nature.

Christian sympathies lie with the Savage, though in a qualified way. To be genuinely brave in a brave new world requires resisting the idolatrous faith in technology and medicine, and such resistance requires the kind of passion exemplified by the Savage. To be genuinely free *and* human requires living dangerously, though not recklessly; that in and through love the risk of being unhappy is accepted. Two qualifications, however, need to be emphasized. First, pain, suffering, and unhappiness are *not* goods to be pursued, but are among the consequences necessarily entailed in the lives of finite and mortal creatures. Second, resisting an idolatrous faith in technology and medicine does not include their wholesale rejection. There is no need to deny that modern technology and medicine have improved the lives of many people, and there is no compelling reason to attempt a nostalgic return to a more primitive age.

Given the second qualifier, it might be asked, So why resist? As was argued in the preceding section, the three principal criticisms of the brave new world of late modernity are a loathing of the body, corruption of desire, and an absence of genuine love. Correcting these deficiencies requires aligning all lesser loves and desires to the love and desire for God, resulting in divided temporal loyalties that must in turn be ordered accordingly. The Controller might respond that all I am doing is joining the Savage in reserving the right to be unhappy, for the love I am championing can only amplify human finitude and mortality along with their attendant pain and suffering. Do not the mobility and autonomy of late modern nomadic life liberate us from this unhappiness? If one must love, direct the sentiment toward oneself and not others.

Enslavement and freedom

What the Controller is offering is not freedom but enslavement. We become enslaved to ourselves, attempting to fulfill insatiable desires. Hence the endless quest for novelty; the new and improved. Within a year or two my new computer will be outdated. This year's vacation must be more adventurous than last year's. Improved medical treatments must be constantly developed to sustain the demand for enhanced performance and longer lives. Late modern nomads are cruel taskmasters that keep themselves perpetually on the move in search of ever new and improved products, services, and experiences.

It was also suggested above that genuine freedom is attained only by consenting to limits. In the absence of definitive limits, the resulting frenetic activity is enslaving, for one is captive to feeding the insatiable appetite of the self-made self. In contrast, affirming the finitude and mortality of our creaturely status provides an underlying order that is the prerequisite of freedom, and that ordering requires us to make choices that both form and constrain who we are and what we do. To use a trivial example, if I walk on the baseball field wearing shoulder pads and carrying a golf club, I have created a novel experience, but I am not playing baseball. To play baseball I must obey the rules that limit what I can do. I cannot tackle an opposing player running the bases, nor can I tee the ball on home plate and swing away. Moreover, if I choose to play baseball, then I also choose not to play football or golf. It is only in submitting to the defining and delimiting rules of baseball that I am free to play it.

Similarly, we also make choices and abide by rules that shape *and* limit who we are and what we do. We choose, either explicitly or implicitly, our friends and what career we pursue; we choose whether or not to marry; and we choose whether or not to love and serve God. If I choose this person to be a friend, then I foreclose the possibility of another person being a friend; when I chose to be a teacher it meant I could not be a farmer or big-game hunter. When I chose a life of marriage I foreclosed a life of singleness; in affirming my baptism I disavowed serving idols. Each of these choices also requires that I submit to certain rules: to speak truthfully rather than flatter my friends; to teach my students what is true rather than false; to be faithful to my wife; to worship God and forgive my neighbors. In the constraints imposed by these choices and rules, I am freed to be (or more accurately strive to be with God's mercy and grace) a trusted friend, a diligent teacher, a good husband, a faithful Christian.

This message of freedom in limitation is a hard sell in a nomadic culture that is devoted to keeping every option open and unburdening oneself of constraints. Am I not advocating a path of resistance that few will choose to follow? Perhaps, for the situation is more challenging than I have portrayed. I am attempting to criticize and resist a culture that has formed and shaped who I am and what I do in profound ways from which I cannot escape; I am trying to assess late modern nomadic culture as a late modern nomad. Perhaps I am so deeply embedded in this culture that I cannot think very clearly or critically about it, much less offer any effective resistance. This is especially the case in respect to technology in general and medicine in particular. In living out the imperative to "love yourself," late modern nomads also become the servants of the technologies they use to satisfy their voracious wants. The machines, instruments, and medicine they employ to master nature and human nature manipulate them in turn. The technology and medical treatments deployed to enhance their mobility and autonomy make them increasingly dependent upon further technological and medical developments, thereby effectively decreasing their freedom. And by and large, as late modern nomads we are unaware of this vicious circle.

Grant has stated the dilemma rather well: "When we represent technology to ourselves as an array of neutral instruments invented by human beings and under human control, we are expressing a kind of common sense, but it is a common sense from within the very technology we are attempting to represent."[25] The culture that technology helps construct encases its inhabitants, disabling them to make critical judgments about it; it is like trying to think about altruism by gazing incessantly in a mirror. Being deeply embedded within this nomadic culture is altering how and what we value. Again in Grant's trenchant words: "The coming to be of technology has required changes in what we think is good, what we think good is, how we conceive sanity and madness, justice and injustice, rationality and irrationality, beauty and ugliness."[26]

The work of Albert Borgmann may be used to help interpret and resist (or better, subvert) at least some of the more egregious effects of these revaluations. In his book *Technology and the Character of Contemporary Life*, he describes what he calls "the device paradigm."[27] Goods and services are reduced to commodities that are easily and readily consumed—devices well suited for highly mobile and autonomous individuals. Borgmann draws two implications from this commodification. The first ramification is shoddy work. Commodities and devices are designed to be used by individuals pursuing new and novel experiences. Consequently, there is a demand for products that are easily disposed of and replaced rather than maintained and repaired. The second implication is that the ravenous consumption of commodities and the ubiquitous presence of devices change the patterns of daily life, particularly within the household. Late modern nomads, for instance, tend to graze rather than dine. Increased mobility changes where, when, and how meals are prepared and eaten. More often than not they are eaten on the run, in a fast-food restaurant, or on the coffee table in front of the television rather than at the dining room table at regular hours throughout the day. Food is a commodity to be consumed quickly rather than also providing an occasion for leisurely conversation with friends or family. The introduction of other devices has also changed household living patterns. With central heating, for instance, a family need not gather together around the living room hearth as the only source of heat but can be scattered throughout various rooms. By extension the device paradigm also alters broader social interactions. I can go shopping for a computer, for example, without ever seeing another person; a student may rarely if ever enter a classroom by taking online courses.

A third, more disturbing, implication may be added to Borgmann's list: the commodification of human relationships and bodies. Are not friendship, marriage, family, and even God coming to be perceived as commodities to be consumed? And in turn, are not the persons comprising these relationships coming to be seen as items that can be disposed of and replaced as needed? In addition, are not the bodies of others perceived increasingly as resources to be utilized in such instances as organ transplantation and embryonic stem cells? And in turn, are not one's body and the bodies of others coming to be seen as artifacts to be crafted into what one wants them to become, as in the cases, respectively, of physical and cognitive enhancements and the selection of offspring based on genetic criteria?

It may be objected that the problem is not technology and medicine, but a failure of personal responsibility. A person can choose whether or not to buy a new computer or television, and she or he can choose when to turn them on and off. One can choose whether to dine or to graze. People can choose to maintain their relationships rather than disposing of and replacing them. A person can choose whether or not to enhance his or her physical and cognitive capabilities, and decide to select or refrain from selecting genetic characteristics of offspring. If late moderns are selfish, shallow, and fragmented, they have no one to blame but themselves. To cast the blame upon an abstract device paradigm is simply an attempt to shirk personal responsibility.

There is much to be said in favor of this objection. People can and do make choices and should assume responsibility for their consequences. Yet the notion of choice invoked is misleading in respect to the purported freedom that choosing implies. Ironically, choice itself becomes a commodity in late modern cultures, and any commodity can only be consumed in a limited number of ways, thereby requiring consumers to adjust our lives accordingly. The introduction of a new technology inevitably alters the patterns of daily life, because it invariably changes the choices that must be made. To use a commonplace example, when I bought a mobile phone, I justified my choice on the basis that I would use it only for emergencies. I now routinely ring my wife from the grocery store to ask her where the tarragon is located. I do make choices about how I use my mobile phone, but those choices are shaped and constrained by the device itself. To not be readily accessible to those who need to contact me is, to a large extent, to misuse the technology. The very availability of new technologies and medical treatments shapes their use and applications, especially in respect to giving one or one's offspring a competitive advantage. Or again in the words of Grant: "To put the matter crudely: when we represent technology to ourselves through its own common sense we think of ourselves as picking and choosing in a supermarket, rather than within the analogy of the package deal."[28] We cannot really pick and choose, for the commodities and devices that make up the fabric of contemporary life impose upon us the ways they should be used.

Faithful resistance

If Grant is right, isn't resistance futile? Although Grant's analysis is essentially correct, he goes a bit too far. In short, a package deal can be subverted, provided that one's desires and loves are ordered to a greater purpose. One can make choices that resist the self-oriented logic and rationale of the device paradigm. Instead of allowing our choices to be dictated by the imperative of "love yourself," we can obey the command to love God and neighbor and make our choices accordingly. In other words, we can choose to remain focused on what is genuinely good. In this respect we may return to Borgmann to gain some hints for how Christians might be genuinely brave in resisting the more troubling features of the late modern world.[29] In response to commodifying tendencies, for instance, Borgmann contends that the "counterforce to the rule of technology is the dedication to focal things and practices."[30] What are focal things and practices? Defined succinctly: "Generally, a focal thing is concrete and of a commanding presence. A focal practice is the decided, regular, and normally communal devotion to a focal thing."[31] A focal thing is not a commodity to be consumed, but an objective reality that shapes the values and behavior of those whose attention is seized by its presence. A focal practice consists of acts that express and perform the convictions and behavior that are formed by those devoted to the focal thing. Although a focal thing commands the attention of its devotees, it is not self-sufficient, requiring the care and attentiveness of practitioners. Focal things and practices embody a formative tradition against which the character and virtues of its adherents are conformed.

Borgmann uses family dining to illustrate the formative influence of focal things and practices. "The great meal of the day, be it at noon or in the evening, is a focal event par excellence. It gathers the scattered family around the table."[32] Those gathered at the table are not present merely to consume food. The meal is a focal point of activity, binding the family together through common traditions and practices. Ingredients are carefully chosen and prepared in following favorite recipes. The table is properly set, and later the tableware is washed and stored. Family members adjust their schedules to be present at the prescribed time, and they focus their attention in participating in the conversation around the table. Moreover, the meal links the family to a larger network of social relationships. When guests are present there are rules of hospitality to follow, and the meal itself should inspire thanksgiving for the efforts of farmers, cooks, dishwashers, and crafters who make the meal possible. As a focal activity, such a meal is the "enactment of generosity and gratitude, the affirmation of mutual and perhaps religious obligations," a far cry from the "social and cultural anonymity of a fast-food outlet."[33] Most importantly, the meal reinforces that those formed by the practices of the dinner table are finite and temporal creatures. They are dependent upon bountiful harvests, and unlike the easy and incessant consumption of packaged commodities, the communal meal is bracketed by time; it has a designated beginning, middle, and end.

The "culture of the table"[34] is emblematic of larger forms of religious, philosophical, and moral discourse that provide a potent counterforce to the device paradigm. Why is such a counterforce needed? In answering this question it is important to emphasize that Borgmann is not antitechnology. By invoking the culture of the table he is *not* grasping for a nostalgic fantasy of a bygone, less frenetic age. Rather, the discourse generated by focal things and practices is needed to bring about a "principled and fruitful reform of technology."[35] This reform is especially urgent as late modern nomadic culture gathers momentum in shaping who its inhabitants are and what they aspire to become. As described previously, this formation is now taking place in a highly mobile world without permanent borders and boundaries, subject to endless and temporary construction of varying desires, values, and relationships. Yet in the process of creating this brave new world, its inhabitants are also recreating themselves as self-made selves. Consequently, the prospect of humans transforming themselves into posthumans cannot be precluded, for there is no compelling reason why it is good to remain human.

If Christians are to resist this prospect, then, an important focal thing is remaining human. Honoring this commanding presence requires them to affirm their embodiment as a good gift to be received with gratitude instead of a curse to be despised. To make this affirmation also requires that they embrace their finitude and mortality and to order their desires in accordance with these constraints. Two focal practices suggest themselves in undertaking this task.

The first focal practice is *Eucharist*. As Borgmann has observed, for Christians it is but a "short step" from the culture of the table to the sacrament of the Lord's Table.[36] For Christians, the Eucharist may serve as a focal practice in resisting the nomadic temptations of late modernity. The Eucharist reveals and enacts the commanding presence of the incarnate God that captures attentiveness and engagement. Through requisite and regular acts of confession, repentance, forgiveness, and amendment of life, the Lord's Table becomes the centerpiece of a celebrative community. These requisite acts in turn shape the church as a repentant, forgiven, forgiving, and sanctified community. Moreover, the materially ordinary bread and wine affirm the finite and mortal nature of creaturely existence; in partaking of Christ's body and blood Christians affirm natural limits and the limits of their human nature. Yet the Lord's Table is also an eschatological banquet, anticipating eternal fellowship in the fullness of time; at this table there is a foretaste of creation's destiny in Christ. In the Eucharist, a time and space is made for affirming and ordering the priority of our loves.

45

The second focal practice is *Sabbath*. The Sabbath is most often associated with a day of rest. Yet the Sabbath is more than rest; it is not merely a diversion from the workweek. Keeping Sabbath requires that we refrain from all other activities to focus attention on what is truly good, on the love of God that orders all lesser loves. Keeping Sabbath, then, requires a place to stop for a while. The problem is not the mobility of the contemporary world, but its perpetual motion. The Christian tradition has never been opposed to mobility. Jesus was an itinerant, and St. Paul was always on a missionary journey. Christians are a restless people because they are never quite at home in the world, but this does not make them nomads. They are, as St. Augustine recognized, sojourners. People on a sojourn do not wander aimlessly but settle down in a place for a while, waiting for their Lord in particular locales. To keep Sabbath is to find a place wherever we may be, to pause and order our loves and desires.

Both of these focal practices are admittedly simple, but it is their elegant simplicity that enables the practitioner to resist the commonsense logic of the late modern nomadic culture. Embracing these practices requires us to alter our lives to accommodate them, not vice versa. To celebrate the Eucharist requires Christians to gather together in a particular place at a specified time. The sacrament cannot, for instance, be received over the Internet at one's convenience. Keeping Sabbath requires a single-minded devotion to prayer and reflection to the exclusion of other activities. Sabbath cannot be kept while on the run, or as part of a multitasking scheme. Both practices also require cutting off access to the devices that shape the patterns of daily life. The Eucharist and Sabbath both provide a place and time of sojourning that resist the mobile and autonomous impulses of nomadic life.

It may be objected that these focal practices are not needed to gain a respite from the device paradigm that I decry. A person can choose to turn off the gadgets for a period of time each day, creating for himself or herself a protected personal time and space. Yet such a strategy reinforces the paradigm's pervasive influence, for it entails creating one more device to manage and deflect the intrusion of other devices. Rather, the focal practices of Eucharist and Sabbath require sequestering oneself in a time and space from distracting devices so that one's attention is focused upon God. Moreover, they are not practices that can be performed in solitude by an autonomous individual, but only in communion with others, for they are practices that focus attention on the love of God *and* neighbor.

In this chapter I used Huxley's *Brave New World* to assist Christian theological reflection on the formative roles that technology and medicine play in the late modern world. It is not a hopelessly wicked world, but there are tendencies that need to be resisted. There is, for instance, nothing inherently wrong with using medicine to help people live long, healthy, and productive lives, but when the relatively good desire of greater longevity becomes the object of one's overarching love, it distorts both the ordering of desire and the practice of medicine. The temptation to be resisted is desiring good things badly. Hence the need for resistance, for to be genuinely brave in the brave new world of late modernity is to remain focused on what is genuinely good, so that long, healthy, and productive lives might be a blessing, not only for oneself but also for others. If as finite and mortal creatures humans isolate themselves from one another and direct their love toward themselves to lessen the risk of vulnerability and suffering, they settle for being something less than human. It is precisely this risk that makes the bonds of love and affection possible, and it is these fragile bonds that enable humans to become the kind of creatures God intends them to be. In his letter to the Romans, St. Paul makes the enigmatic observation that we are awaiting the redemption of our bodies. That redemption is a gift of grace to be anticipated and received rather than a summons to undertake a construction project; it is to be embraced by the Word made flesh, and not to engineer flesh into data.

As has been intimated, medicine, in tandem with technology, has effectively become the salvific faith of late moderns. The following chapters, to use one of Grant's favorite words, *enucleate* ("to extract the kernel of a nut, the seed of a tree"[37]) this faith, both to test the adequacy of the confidence being placed in it and to gain clarity regarding the contemporary context in which Christians are called to proclaim their counterfaith in the incarnate Word.

2

A Theological Reflection on
Reproductive Medicine

As late moderns we turn increasingly to medicine in ordering human reproduction. We employ various treatments to prevent or assist conception, and we are developing a greater capacity for preventing or selecting the characteristics of offspring. The ethical issues accompanying various reproductive technologies are well known (for example, contraception, donated gametes, surrogacy, abortion, preimplantation genetic diagnosis), and I do not revisit them in this chapter.[1] Rather, I reflect theologically on our steady attempts to "medicalize" procreation, and suggest some implications this reflection might pose for the church's ministry.

Is Rachel's Lament Our Lament?

A few poignant lines from the Bible capture the plight of an infertile couple. Rachel pleads to her husband, Jacob, "Give me children, or I'll die!" Jacob replies angrily, "Am I in the place of God, who has kept you from having children?"[2] This brief exchange barely contains the underlying and powerful emotions: bitter disappointment, mutual recriminations, and a sense of powerlessness in the face of

natural forces beyond the couple's control. We may assume that we
share with Rachel and Jacob a common set of emotional reactions.
We can reach back across the broad chasm of time separating us
to feel their pain and empathize with their disappointment. Such
an assumption is premature, however, for there is more to the story
that must be told.

Rachel and her sister, Leah, are *both* married to Jacob. Although
Jacob favors Rachel, she is "barren," whereas Leah bears her husband
four sons before she herself becomes unable to bear more children.
It is at this point that Rachel, out of jealousy, pleads with Jacob to
give her children. Not satisfied with his retort that there is nothing
he can do, she gives him her maid, who, on behalf of Rachel, bears
Jacob two sons. Not to be outdone, Leah also gives Jacob her maid,
"as a wife," who gives birth to two more sons. But the story does
not end here. Both sisters take a medicinal herb, and Leah bears two
additional sons and a daughter, while Rachel at last gives birth to
a son, Joseph.[3]

The purpose for dwelling on the lurid details of this story is *not*
to imply that even in antiquity unsophisticated methods, such as
surrogate wives and medicinal herbs, were used to remedy the pain
of childlessness. The only difference is that we now have more sophisticated techniques to solve a perennial problem. To the contrary,
what must be highlighted is a *social context* significantly different
from our own: Rachel's plea is uttered within a polygamous and
patriarchal household. As Jacob's wife, her role is to perpetuate her
husband's lineage through the birth of sons. Indeed, the very purpose
and meaning of procreation are tied directly to the fate of Jacob's
household, for this is the story of the origin of the nation of Israel
through the twelve tribes (sons) of Jacob.[4] If Rachel cannot give her
husband sons either through her own body or through the body of a
substitute, then she has no future to envision and embrace. In short,
Rachel's lament is one of an unfulfilled destiny.

But is Rachel's lament also our lament? Do we use reproductive
medicine to fulfill our destinies? Or to pose the question from an
alternative angle, do we think differently about children and what it
means to be a parent than did our ancestors in the faith? If so, does
this difference shed any light on how we are coming to perceive and
use our growing ability to manipulate reproductive processes? To

begin answering these questions, we must turn our attention to the background of our so-called secular age.

Reproduction, Freedom, and Medicine

We are coming to perceive the parent–child relationship within a moral framework that may be characterized as "reproductive freedom" or "procreative liberty."[5] The essential principle is that every person has a fundamental right either to reproduce or to refrain from reproducing. Few, if any, restrictions should be imposed or tolerated that would impede individuals from exercising this right. Moreover, should individuals choosing to reproduce encounter any physical limitations (such as infertility) or social inequalities (such as unavailable partners), they should have access to technologies, as well as a right to collaborate with other individuals (such as gamete donors or surrogates), to obtain a child.

A second tenet is that since individuals have a right to reproduce, then they also have a right to obtain a desirable child. A parent should not be obligated to care for a severely ill or disabled child if such a condition could be prevented prior to birth. This does not reflect, necessarily, a callous attitude, but rather a presumably humane impulse to prevent unnecessary suffering. In addition, as more sophisticated techniques are developed, parents should also have the right to select or enhance certain characteristics they find desirable in offspring.

For the purpose of this chapter, there are two observations to be noted regarding these basic principles of reproductive freedom. First, proponents of procreative liberty assert that although individuals should be free to use reproductive medicine to obtain a child, they should also be under no compulsion to do so. An infertile couple, for example, should be free to contract the services of a surrogate, while a couple carrying the recessive genes for cystic fibrosis should not be compelled to screen embryos prior to implantation in order to prevent the birth of a child with the disease.

Yet individuals desiring to reproduce must be free to exercise various reproductive options, even options that other individuals might find objectionable.[6] Consequently, medicine plays a growing role in implementing reproductive freedom, both through assisting reproduction (through such techniques as artificial insemination, in vitro fertilization, and surrogacy) and through exerting greater "quality control" by preventing the birth of severely ill or disabled children (through such techniques as prenatal diagnosis and preimplantation genetic diagnosis). Providing an expanding array of options enhances the *freedom* of people pursuing their respective reproductive interests, thereby benefiting a growing range of individuals.

Second, proponents of procreative liberty do not assert or assume a common, much less normative, understanding of the parent–child relationship. Reproductive medicine may be used to obtain a child that may or may not be genetically related to the parent(s). A single, infertile man, for example, could use "donated" gametes in conjunction with in vitro fertilization and a surrogate to obtain a child of "his own." Thus a parent is a person who freely (and successfully) asserts the *will* to obtain a child. John Robertson, a leading advocate of reproductive freedom, defines a parent as a "commissioner" who works with willing "collaborators" for the purpose of obtaining a child. Persons initiating and overseeing a reproductive project are the true parents, for "they were the prime movers in bringing all the parties together to produce the child," relying on the promises or contracts with the "gamete providers and gestator" to accomplish this goal.[7]

It may be objected that this portrayal of reproductive freedom as the moral background for how we are coming to perceive the meaning of parenthood, as well as children, is misleading, because it represents a fringe rather than a mainline outlook. The vast majority of couples do not use reproductive medicine in the manner described above, and even many of those who do would be offended by our characterizing them as commissioners overseeing a collaborative reproductive project.

The objection, however, reinforces the basic tenets of reproductive freedom, namely, that individuals are free to use or *not* to use reproductive medicine in whatever ways they choose. No one is compelled to commission or collaborate in a reproductive project. Yet those wishing to employ assisted reproduction or quality control techniques should be free to do so. Consequently, *all* reproductive methods are subsumed into a framework of reproductive freedom, because they all share the common objective of obtaining a child. The only difference between assisted and natural reproduction is one of scale: the vast majority of couples pursuing the latter have chosen to restrict the scope of collaboration while opting for a "low-tech" method. In the end, any method used to become a parent involves the will to obtain a child.

To return, then, to our earlier question: Is Rachel's lament our lament? Apparently not, for, unlike her unfulfilled destiny, our disappointment centers on a frustrated will. In some relatively rare instances the despair of childlessness may center on the impending demise of a husband's bloodline, but more commonly reproductive medicine is employed to alleviate the grief of individuals unable to have a child of their own or who carry deleterious genes that can be passed on to offspring. Theologically, how are we to come to terms with how this centrality of the will is coming to define the parent–child relationship? Should Christians be troubled and wary, or to the contrary, are these developments in reproductive medicine to be welcomed and celebrated?

Theological Themes

If the will plays *the* central role in what it now means to be a parent, then two obvious responses suggest themselves. On the one hand, any technique displacing natural processes or involving the destruction of embryos could be rejected for a variety of moral or theological reasons. It could be argued, for example, that it is wrong to use assisted reproduction and many quality control techniques because they require the willful destruction of embryos. Consequently, Christians should not use most, if not all, reproductive technologies. Although it is understandable that couples will be deeply disappointed, their only recourse is to adopt, provide foster care, or remain childless while redirecting their generative impulse through acts of charity that help disadvantaged children.[8] The pastoral response is essentially to help individuals deal with their disappointment and perhaps assist them in investigating the limited range of permissible options that are available to them.

On the other hand, it may be argued that the method used to obtain a child is morally irrelevant so long as prospective parents are motivated by a sincere love for children. Consequently, the full range of techniques offered by reproductive medicine may be deployed. Reproductive technologies are simply useful tools that assist individuals in expressing a genuine and commendable love for children.[9] The pastoral response may be characterized as helping prospective parents sort out which, among the many, options are compatible with their beliefs and values, and then supporting them in whatever choices they make.

Both of these options, however, are insufficient *if* our reproductive decisions are to reflect faithfully our lives as Christians. The first option places an unwarranted emphasis on so-called natural reproductive processes that should remain inviolate. Yet such a stance is incompatible with other medical procedures that Christians endorse and employ routinely to intervene in other natural processes (such as inoculations or suppressing the immune system in conjunction with organ transplantations or treating rare forms of arthritis). Although the church's pastoral ministry should help individuals accept the (often unwanted) limits of their lives as embodied creatures, this is not synonymous with stoic resignation or silent acquiescence to fate.

The other option not only discounts bodily limitations as having any moral or theological significance but tends to portray them merely as irritating obstacles that should be overcome if they prevent us from achieving a good goal such as the love for children. More troubling is a strong tendency toward reducing children to a means of self-fulfillment. Children help their parents become more whole and complete persons. Although a love for children presupposes sacrifice and self-giving on the part of parents, parental responsibilities must somehow be incorporated "into the self-fulfillment picture"[10] if they are to inspire sincere commitment. Yet a genuine parental love must surely encompass certain qualities other than what individuals seeking their own fulfillment choose to express. What is lacking in this option is any larger understanding of the parent–child relationship against which the suitability of various methods for "obtaining" children can be assessed. In the absence of such a standard, parental self-fulfillment becomes by default the overriding consideration.

A preferable pastoral response is to offer *theological companion-ship*.[11] At its most basic level, such companionship enables Christians to form and live out their lives in line with core theological beliefs and convictions. In respect to procreation and child rearing, it requires asking such questions as: What does it mean to be a parent and child in light of the Triune God who creates, sustains, and redeems our lives? What does it mean to be parents and children together as Christians within the community of faith? What must we do, or refrain from doing, to remain faithful to these formative beliefs and convictions? Thus, the very nature of theological companionship requires that we pay close attention to the *means* or *methods* of reproductive options that are now open to us, the *social contexts* in which the parent–child relationship is formed and lived out, and the *purposes* for which Christians might be called to become parents.

Attempting to answer these questions in any depth is beyond the scope of this chapter. But some trajectories for further inquiry can be suggested by exploring briefly the theological themes of the body, hospitality, and witness.

Body

Christians believe that humans have been created in God's image and likeness. It needs to be acknowledged adamantly that their status as such creatures is implausible apart from their bodies. Christians especially must emphasize the body when thinking about procreation, because of a profound ambivalence pervading our late modern culture, reflecting an underlying and destructive dualism. We have presumably constructed a society in which we are no longer ashamed or unduly modest about the human body, and as the fitness movement demonstrates, many of us expend much time and attention in taking care of our bodies. Yet alongside this fascination with our bodies is a thinly veiled repulsion as reflected in lifestyles promoting unhealthy diets and inadequate rest, or in desperate struggles to maintain a youthful appearance.

How may we account for these apparent contradictions? It has much to do with how we are coming to shape and express a sense of personal identity. In short, not many of us would say something like, "I am my body." Rather, we tend to identify who we are in terms of a mind, spirit, or will, providing a disembodied starting point for projecting our goals and aspirations. It is the pursuit of these goals and aspirations that in turn expresses who we are and who we hope to become. In some instances our bodies are useful instruments for fulfilling our dreams, while in many other instances they are annoying and frustrating obstacles.

Yet when Christians speak about the body, they must take care about what they say lest they fall into a similar trap. Even such a seemingly innocuous phrase as, "I have a body," implies that bodies are property we own and may do with as we will. But our lives belong to God, and it is in and through our bodies that God entrusts to us the gift and loan of life. Even attaching the qualifying "embodied" to our status as "creatures" is inadequate if it implies that ultimately the body is but a temporary container for the more important soul.[12] It is not just the soul (or mind or will) that God loves and redeems, but the whole, full, and complete creature that bears and embodies the divine image and likeness. In this respect, it is important to remember that for many of our ancestors in the faith it was the resurrection of the body, and *not* the survival of a disembodied soul, that seized their attention.

In providing theological companionship, our status as bodied creatures should not be overlooked. It may at first seem odd to invoke such a plea, for reproductive medicine is most often employed in response to dysfunctional biological processes. Is the body in these instances not center stage? Not in the full sense of the word, for in assisting reproduction we must necessarily reduce bodies to smaller parts and functions to accomplish the goal of obtaining a child. Thus, it is of little concern, for example, whose womb or whose gametes are used.

I am *not* suggesting that fertility should be the ultimate determinative factor for defining parenthood, but neither should bodily factors and limitations be dismissed or discounted in a cavalier manner. What is at stake is something more than repairing or utilizing reproductive processes and materials, for reproductive technologies are employed and, in turn, shape the social contexts in which relationships between parents and children are established. These contexts are not simply separate or cut off from human biology, because it is as bodied creatures that humans worship and bear witness to God, form their friendships and communities, and, most importantly, procreate and educate children. The issue, however, is not so much that reproductive medicine enables us to intervene in natural processes, but to what extent certain reproductive methods help or hinder us from welcoming children into these formative contexts.

Hospitality

Christianity is a social and relational faith. Christians worship and serve a God whose unity is expressed through three persons in community. St. Paul portrays the church as the body of Christ, comprised of various parts, each with their unique gift or function, but dysfunctional in isolation from each other.[13] Monastics withdrawing from temporal affairs more often than not do so within communities, and the relatively few hermits seek solitude to devote their time to praying for the world. We become the kind of people God intends us to be in relationship with others.

Traditionally, Christians have presumed that the parent–child relationship should be formed within a household, or *oikos*. It is from this Greek term *oikos* that the word *economy* is derived, connoting a setting or context that is particularly well suited or well equipped to achieve a certain purpose or end. It is within a household that the parent–child relationship properly unfolds. Outside this *oikos* the roles of parent and child are stripped of normative meaning, for they share unique bonds of affection, mutuality, and fidelity that cannot be replicated in any other social setting.[14] Thus, to think about reproduction in the context of laboratories is not synonymous with thinking about procreation in the setting of a household, or *oikos*.

There are two important observations to note regarding households: First, they are largely comprised of people not of one's choosing. We do not choose our parents, nor do we choose our children (though we may choose initially to become parents). The members of a household belong together in a relationship that is mutual, but largely involuntary and ideally unconditional. Children and parents are usually not required to pass entrance exams before being admitted to a family.

Second, households are *not* secluded enclaves, providing a private haven in an otherwise heartless world. Rather, if the economy of an *oikos* is properly ordered, it draws its members out toward greater spheres of friendship and affiliation, becoming a base of hospitality.[15] Yet if households are to offer hospitality, they must first provide hospitable environments for their members.

Does our growing recourse to reproductive medicine tend to make households more or less hospitable to children? Although any sweeping generalizations should be avoided, we may nonetheless offer some words of caution: as procreation becomes increasingly medicalized, there is a corresponding tendency to perceive children as the outcomes of reproductive projects. If parents can be perceived as commissioners, then it is also not unreasonable to perceive the finished product as an artifact of their reproductive will. This is particularly the case with respect to quality control techniques. Parenthood takes on a highly tentative character, because only embryos or fetuses meeting certain criteria are selected.[16] Hospitality is not freely extended but is withheld until the tests are passed.

To counter this tendency, Christians should insist that parenthood is *not* a project to be undertaken (or a right or entitlement to be exercised) but is a *sacred trust* that is given by God. It is in the hospitable reception of that trust that we bear witness to the source and end of our faith.

Witness

Parents bear witness to God by welcoming children into hospitable households, and given the nature of procreation and child rearing, it is inescapably a bodily witness. This is portrayed in traditional Christian teaching that children are the fruition of the one-flesh unity of marriage. It is through the totality of their relationship that a couple brings into being a new life. Thus, parents and children share a fundamental equality as God's bodied creatures, a relationship, it should be noted, that is not shared by a commissioner and an artifact. In this respect, Oliver O'Donovan offers the salutary reminder that children are properly begotten rather than made.[17]

This does not imply, however, that a Christian understanding of the parent/child relationship can be reduced to biology or genetics. Parents do not have children of "their own," nor do children belong to their parents. Rather, children belong to God and are entrusted to the care of parents. Consequently, the church may without any sense of contradiction affirm children as the fruition of the one-flesh unity of their parents, while also affirming with equal conviction the vocation of adoptive and foster parents.

Moreover, this is also why no blanket commendation or condemnation can be thrown over reproductive medicine. Although the reproductive potential and limits of the human body are not the overriding consideration for defining parenthood, neither can they be easily dismissed or ignored. Consequently, each technique should be assessed in terms of the extent to which it either enables or distorts the parental witness. It is one thing to employ these techniques in pursuing a reproductive project and quite another matter for using them to prepare a couple to receive the gift of a child that God entrusts to their care.[18]

In this respect, it is right to insist that a love for children should be our overriding consideration. But it is a love that is expressed through *both* the potential and limits of our lives as bodied creatures, and thus the methods employed in becoming a parent are not irrelevant. It is not solely a love that empowers our will and self-fulfillment, but a divine and self-giving love embodied in the parental witness, and we cannot escape or ignore the destiny toward which a parental witness points.

Back to Rachel: Destiny and Ministry

It was suggested above that Rachel's lament is not our lament. Her lament stemmed from an unfulfilled destiny, while we bemoan a frustrated will. Yet our frustration comes from unfulfilled aspirations, and what we aspire to must surely point toward some larger destiny, however vague or implicit it might be. The critical issue, then, is whether our use of reproductive medicine bears witness to a true or false destiny.

It is instructive to recall that the earliest Christians preferred continent singleness over marriage and family. This preference did not simply reflect a belief that sexual intercourse was sinful or shameful, but that sexual renunciation was itself a witness. Unlike today, underpopulation, rather than overpopulation, was the pressing issue capturing public attention. Due to high infant mortality rates, it is estimated that every woman within the Roman Empire had to give birth at least five times to maintain a stable population. Rome's destiny rested squarely on its offspring. Marriage, procreation, and child rearing were not personal options, but public duties.[19] In refusing to perform these duties, the early Christians indicated that they had nothing at stake in Rome's false destiny. Rather, they placed their hope in the future of God's kingdom that would not be inherited by flesh and blood, and also refused to allow their bodies to be used as resources for fulfilling imperial ambition.

There is no clear parallel between the context of the early church and our late modern circumstances. Recent developments in reproductive medicine have largely not been driven by a desire to secure our destiny through offspring. These developments, however, are forcing us to redefine what parenthood now means, and it is incumbent upon Christians to be clear about how this redefining may either enable or blunt their faithful witness. They may come to discover that some techniques can assist them in performing faithfully their procreative stewardship, but they should not allow technological potential and efficiency to distort the object of the true hope to which they bear witness.

In the light of reproductive medicine the church is called to offer its theological companionship to help Christians discern what their witness requires of them. A pastoral call in response to a parishioner's recent discovery of infertility or of being a carrier of a potentially deleterious gene that can be passed on to offspring is not the best time to begin offering theological companionship. Rather, it requires an ongoing discernment of how Christian households may more hospitably receive children, and how communities of faith may empower a parental witness to the true destiny in Christ. To explore the relationships among the body, hospitality, and witness may offer a promising starting point for embracing a stewardship of life that God has entrusted to those creatures bearing the divine image and likeness.

3

Are Our Genes Our Fate?

Genomics and Christian Theology

To say that human genetics has captured public attention is to merely state the obvious. The media is saturated with the implications of the letters G, A, T, C. Books about genes, both fiction and nonfiction, often make the top-seller lists. Moviegoers are frightened by the genetic splicing and dicing of mad scientists, and business schools talk about a corporation's DNA. Such magazines as *Newsweek*, *Business Week*, and the *Weekly Standard* report frequently on a wide range of issues, and barely a day goes by that the *New York Times*, *Financial Times*, and *Japan Times* don't make some mention of the latest genetic discovery and its medical or commercial application. It is not unreasonable to say that the human genome has a rising iconic status in late modern culture.

Popular culture is certainly not synonymous with science or medicine, yet some extravagant claims and bad reporting are nonetheless shaping public perceptions. It was publicly pronounced, for instance, that the Human Genome Project was biology's Holy Grail that would reveal what being human means. Headlines have announced the search for or discovery of an immortality gene, a fountain of youth gene, an obesity gene, various good and bad behavior genes, and even a religious gene. These immodest claims, no doubt, make responsible scientists and physicians shudder, but they have nevertheless shaped public expectation of an approaching golden age in which genetically based medicine will enable individuals to live longer, healthier, happier, and more productive lives. Despite the hyperbole, genomics *is*, undoubtedly, transforming how medicine is perceived and practiced.

Both fact and fantasy have consequences, however, for together they influence how research funding is allocated and the investment strategies of aging venture capitalists. More broadly, there is the growing belief that one's health, and therefore longevity, is invariably linked to one's genes. Hence the turn to medicine as the most promising tool for controlling that fate, a turn that might be characterized as religious. Not religious in a formal sense, but more along the lines of what Paul Tillich identifies as "ultimate concern,"[1] or, to paraphrase Martin Luther,[2] where people place their trust is properly the object of their faith and devotion. Arguably, health is becoming, or has already become, the ultimate concern of late moderns, and they therefore place their trust in medicine.

This chapter assesses this religious significance, in terms of how genetically based medicine both enables and disables a faithful response to Jesus Christ as the incarnate God. Or, in more traditional terms, to discern how and to what extent current and anticipated treatments should be received as good gifts in helping humans exercise their stewardship of God's creation, and to discern how and to what extent they are idolatrous and destructive distractions. In undertaking this task I examine the following topics: 1) the relation between genetics and fate; 2) the relation between Christ and destiny; and 3) some implications these relationships have for Christian moral and theological reflection.

Genetics and Fate

When I was young (alas, many years ago), I sometimes frequented establishments where the line, "What's your sign?" was used to initiate edifying conversation with a stranger. Since I am now old and happily married, I no longer visit such places, so I am not familiar with the parlance that is currently in vogue. My hope is that the infamous pick-up line from my generation has fallen out of favor. My fear is that it has been replaced by a more troubling sentiment, something like "How hot is your DNA?"

What is disturbing about both of these questions is their underlying fatalism. It is either stars or genes that determine the future. In many respects the older belief in the stars is an easier burden to bear, for who one is and where one is headed entail the alignment of the universe. Fate is determined by impersonal, cosmic forces beyond a person's control; each individual is simply a cog in a gigantic machine. The new belief in genes, however, is more personal, for each person carries his or her fate in his or her flesh and blood, determined by accidental circumstances of conception and birth. Are there ways to cheat fate? In the past, one could consult a skilled astrologist to either avoid or make the best of ill fortune. Perhaps future generations will consult genetic counselors to achieve a similar end. This is the kind of popular, fatalistic image that Bryan Appleyard evokes when he ponders whether genetics is becoming the new astrology.[3]

Again, there is a difference between popular culture and science and medicine. Moreover, it is these popular perceptions of genetics and medicine where much of the potential moral and political mischief resides. Before examining this mischief, however, the welcomed and anticipated developments in genetic and medical research need to be acknowledged. Great strides have already been made in improving diagnostic precision. Physicians use genetic indications or markers to monitor individuals who are at risk of contracting a range of life-threatening or chronic diseases. Such monitoring can lead to early detection, thereby improving the therapeutic efficacy, for instance, of newly developed drugs. In addition, the benefits of early detection and improved therapies are enhanced by using genetic tests that indicate whether some patients are prone to toxic side effects, or tests predicting the efficacy of a drug such as tamoxifen in treating breast cancer. It is also reasonable to believe that even more effective diagnostic and therapeutic techniques will be developed in the future.

There is nothing inherently objectionable in these recent and anticipated advances; no reason to assume that improved healthcare is somehow contrary to God's will. The prospect of better medical care should be greeted with gratitude, as a good gift that humans may use in exercising their stewardship of God's creation. This promise, however, is also accompanied by peril. A sinister conspiracy does not need to be conjured to recognize the threat. Rather, the effectiveness of improved genetically based diagnostic and therapeutic techniques is also what makes them perilous. The good and ill consequences of these advances are intricately interwoven so that the latter are easy to miss. The growing knowledge of human genomics has seized public attention to such an extent that late moderns are largely unaware of the degree to which this promise is simultaneously shaping *and* distorting their expectations and moral imagination. Consequently, there is a need to step back from this research to gain some perspective and assess both its good and ill effects.

Three examples suffice to illustrate the peril. First, through better diagnosis, medicine is becoming more adept at preventing pain and suffering, which is certainly a good. One application of this preventive strategy, however, is to prevent the development of embryos that are diagnosed as carrying genetic indications of deleterious diseases or disabilities. Using in vitro fertilization (IVF) in combination with preimplantation genetic diagnosis (PGD), for instance, embryos can be tested and selected for implantation. We need not visit the divisive issue of whether or not embryos are persons to admit that this procedure raises some important concerns. Using PGD can prevent pain and suffering, but it accomplishes this goal by preventing the birth of certain types of individuals. Is an implicit message being sent to people with disabilities or chronic conditions that it would have been better if they had not been born? If this procedure is used more extensively over time, is there a risk that society might grow more inhospitable to individuals that are judged to be disabled or chronically ill? Will asserting greater technological control over the qualitative outcomes of reproduction corrode the parent/child relationship? Is the unconditional nature of this relationship being replaced by conditional criteria? More broadly, should one generation assert such formative power over subsequent generations?

Second, therapies used to treat people with debilitating illnesses can, at least in principle, also be employed to enhance the performance of healthy individuals. Again, to identify some important issues there is no need to paint dystopian visions of genetic engineering run amok. At present, for instance, there is no consensus regarding the nontherapeutic uses of pharmaceuticals. Drugs used to treat ADD and encephalitis can also be used to focus one's concentration or decrease the need for sleep. It is anticipated that new drugs being developed to treat muscular dystrophy might also be used to prevent the loss of strength in older people or to enhance the development of muscles without the lethal side effects of steroids.

These applications offer such benefits as increased productivity, and providing a competitive edge in the workplace or sporting arena. More broadly, they can help sustain the mental alertness, independence, and mobility of an aging population, helping seniors avoid isolation and dependence. These applications, however, also weaken the lines separating therapy, prevention, and enhancement. Although these lines have admittedly always been imprecise, the increased ambiguity raises a number of questions. If distribution of these enhancements is determined by market mechanisms will they create the opposite of level playing fields that liberal democratic societies presumably wish to promote? Can the "un-enhanced" compete with the "enhanced"? Will parents be tempted to enhance the mental and physical performance of their children, especially in cultures that urge them to give offspring the best possible start in life? Will the purported ability to increase productivity, preserve mental and physical agility, and protect personal autonomy serve to promote the most cherished values of civil society or exacerbate its worse features? To what extent will this emphasis on enhancing patients transform medical practice, and will this transformation prove good or ill in respect to medicine's core convictions and commitments?

Underlying these issues is the inability of late moderns to answer the question of what constitutes a normative life. In the absence of such a normative account, there is little, if any, consensus regarding how medicine might help or hinder people in living good lives. As was noted in chapter 1, there is a close relationship between humans and technology in constructing their cultures. With the advent of genetic technologies, that relationship is amplified, perhaps even redefined, for they modify the users in a direct manner. It is the extent of this modification that is the question at issue, and how it is answered depends a great deal on what one believes constitutes a good life.

To use a simplistic analogy from baseball, wearing a bigger mitt or wrapping a weak knee is permissible, while corking a bat or using steroids is forbidden. Each of these strategies enhances a player's performance, so why are these acceptable while those are cheating? How one makes this determination depends a lot on what one believes is the purpose of baseball. To stoop to slogans, invoking "It's not whether you win or lose, but how you play the game" prompts a different answer than "Winning is the only thing" to the question of which types of enhancements should be permitted and which forbidden. Likewise, how one answers this question in the "game of life" is largely determined by what is assumed to be the purpose of being human. Is manipulating one's genes "cheating" or an acceptable enhancement?

Third, increased longevity presumably results from improved diagnostic, therapeutic, and preventive techniques and treatments. Again, there is nothing inherently wrong with living longer, healthier, and happier lives. Late moderns, however, may be entertaining a more ambitious agenda, namely, one of perceiving aging itself as a disease that can be treated. And if it can be treated, why can't it be cured? Lest you think me daft or think I spend too much time reading science fiction, the idea of aging as a disease is appearing with some regularity in medical journals, popular science books, and bioethics literature. There are organizations lobbying governments to fund life prolongation research, and a world transhumanist association that promotes technological development to transform human beings into a superior species. Aubrey de Grey personifies this sentiment most succinctly by insisting that mortality is not simply an unfortunate aspect of being human, but is an unmitigated tragedy that can be overcome through engineering.[4] He believes that research and technological advances in human genetics will lead to greatly increased longevity, for in principle there are no set limits on cellular rejuvenation. If cells and genes prove less pliable than hoped, then these limits can be overcome through anticipated advances in nanotechnology and computer science.

The technological feasibility of this ambitious project is not the issue at stake, for it is inspiring a public perception of what being human now means, and what human beings should aspire to become. It is also an emerging perspective that raises questions: if

66

humans come to regard finitude and mortality as tragic conditions to be overcome rather than as definitive features of human life, what will be the good and ill consequences for ordering interpersonal and intergenerational relationships? If death can be held at bay for a greatly extended period of time, will attention shift to survival, both individually and corporately, and away from the well-being of future generations? Will investing more heavily in extended longevity entail that individuals be less invested in reproducing the future through children and grandchildren? Answering these questions will be particularly telling in respect to medicine, for if its principal task becomes one of waging a war against aging, then it must reengineer rather than merely treat its patients. What will medicine become should its purpose be one of overcoming finitude rather than of helping patients come to terms with its constraints?

As medicine grows more adept at utilizing genomics in developing better diagnostic, preventive, therapeutic, and enhancement techniques, its very success is creating a double bind. On the one hand, there is a tacit admission that with respect to physical and mental health a person's fate is largely, though not entirely, determined by his genes, hence the recourse to PGD to prevent pain and suffering. The goal, however, is achieved by preventing the birth of individuals whose quality of life would be so greatly diminished that it is judged to be not worth pursuing in the first place. In this respect, it is acknowledged that the fate associated with a particular collection of genes cannot be fought. On the other hand, late moderns rebel against the very idea of fate. They turn to genetics to enable medicine to wage war against the finite and mortal limits that have been bequeathed to them by their evolutionary legacy as a species. Or in the words of Eric Cohen, "it is apparently part of our genetic code to revolt against our genetic fate."[5] It is because of this double bind that a religious question is now being posed: can medicine use human genes to save people from their genetic fate?

Christ and Destiny

A comprehensive answer to this question is beyond the scope of this chapter, but the basic features of a theological framework may be sketched out by exploring the relation between Christ and destiny. There is a tendency to use *fate* and *destiny* as synonymous terms, yet there is an important difference that needs to be taken into account. We may say that *fate* refers to a future condition that is given, whereas *destiny* is an eventual consequence of a preceding trajectory of decisions or acts. Death, for example, is a fate shared by all humans, whereas how each individual dies is a matter of destiny that largely grows out of adopted lifestyles and responses to varying circumstances. This does not mean that a person constructs a destiny that is subject to her or his absolute control. There are accidental factors to contend with, and issues of good or bad luck; a person may be killed, for instance, simply by being in the wrong place at the wrong time.

More importantly, as George Grant observed, the choices that one makes are akin to a package deal that carries with it a particular destiny that limits and shapes subsequent choices and acts.[6] This formative process is initiated by making a choice that effectively forecloses other possibilities. Marriage, for instance, forecloses the option of being single; choosing one career means that other possibilities cannot be pursued. Moreover, these decisions entail inherent purposes and expectations regarding subsequent acts and behavior. There are certain duties and responsibilities that are requisite to what it means to be a spouse or teacher; marriage requires fidelity and teaching requires veracity.

We may say that a similar pattern exists when a so-called genetic fate is given, either explicitly or implicitly, the status of a destiny. In our genes we confront a power that is beyond our ability to control, and yet we nonetheless attempt to manipulate it to overcome our limits as finite and mortal creatures. Seen in this light, the double bind described above becomes more explicable, for we are committed simultaneously by an imperative to prevent the suffering *and* enhance the latent capabilities that are inherent in our genes. Consequently, it is incumbent upon us to use genomics to sharpen diagnostic precision and improve therapeutic efficacy.

This double bind serves as a reminder that when proximate and penultimate goods are confused with final and ultimate ends, false or idolatrous expectations emerge. Marriage, knowledge, and health are penultimate goods, but they become distorted and disfigured when granted an ultimacy they do not deserve. If we come to believe that spouses, teachers, or physicians can somehow save us, we will be bitterly disappointed, thereby stripping marriage, education, or medicine of their innate but limited goodness. It is only in light of *the* Good that we value lesser or penultimate goods in a proper manner.

For Christians, this ultimate Good is God, and consequently, their destiny is Christ. Moreover, this destiny is made known in and through the incarnation, the Word made flesh. In becoming a human being, Jesus Christ, as the second person of the Triune God, took on the attributes of a finite and mortal creature. Thus, the destiny of creation and its creatures has been fused with that of their Creator and Redeemer. This message is amplified in the abbreviated creed recited or sung by Christians when they celebrate the Eucharist: Christ has died. Christ is risen. Christ will come again. As a human being, Jesus experienced suffering and death. He died on the cross, and his corpse was placed in a tomb. Thus, the gospel offers no escape from finite and mortal limits. What it does proclaim is that death does not have the final word. Jesus Christ is raised from the dead into the eternal life of God, and that same destiny awaits finite and mortal creatures with whom he shares a bond, for the fate *and* destiny of creation and its creatures are in Christ.

Two pertinent observations can be made regarding this admittedly abbreviated description of the incarnation. First, it affirms humans as embodied, finite, and mortal creatures. There is nothing inherently wrong, evil, or tragic in the fact that humans grow old and die. They are not saved from their finitude and mortality; rather, they are the definitive features of what it means to be human. Christ did not cheat death on Easter Sunday but vindicated creation by reconciling the finite with the infinite, and the mortal with the eternal. It is instructive to remember in this regard that early Christians did not place their hope solely in the survival of the immortal soul, but also in the resurrection of the body, for salvation does not consist of liberating the soul from the body but incorporating the whole person into the eternal life of God. How, then, might genomics help medicine to affirm human finitude and mortality instead of warring against them?

Second, it is as embodied, and therefore necessarily finite and mortal, creatures that humans fulfill the two great commands to love God and neighbor. Such love is therefore necessarily partial and imperfect, because it is also temporal. Consequently, the love humans are commanded to exhibit is not a result of their own initiative, but a response to God's initiative. It is because God, as complete and perfect love, first loved humans that they are in turn enjoined and empowered to love their neighbors, particularly those who are in need. It is important to stress in this regard that the neighbors we are commanded to love are finite and mortal creatures, embodying the inherent fragility and vulnerability that such a status implies. Medicine is an important means of exhibiting the love of neighbor, for it simultaneously provides relief for and fellowship with those who are suffering.[7] Medicine not only is an institution dedicated to healing the sick but also represents the civil community's commitment that the sick shall not be abandoned. Medical care is simultaneously an act of *caritas* (charity) and hospitality, modeling Jesus's twin roles of healer and suffering servant. Jesus not only healed the sick but kept company with them as well.

Theological Reflection

Does all this theological rhetoric make any real difference in deliberating on the host of ethical issues related to genomics and medicine? It does, or at least can, provided that it does not attempt to specify the content of laws and policies governing research or providing access to treatment, but by informing a moral vision that underlies such laws and policies. Three maxims derived from the preceding theological discussion may serve to illustrate this formative influence.

First, *medicine should use genomics to help patients come to terms with their finitude and mortality rather than overcome them.* The Human Genome Project has disclosed that in respect to DNA, human beings are simultaneously wondrously complex and elegantly simple creatures. They are simple in that they do not have nearly as many genes as was first assumed, indeed not many more than most other animals. In many respects they have much in common with hamsters. Humans are complex beings, however, in that their

70

limited genes interact in ways that produce sophisticated creatures with the capability of being highly inquisitive and creative. In many respects, they share nothing in common with the lives of hamsters (other than perhaps spending a great deal of time running in a variety of symbolic wheels).

It would seem that the combination of simplicity and complexity should inspire in humans a sense of profound awe and humility. Yet the response has been more of bewilderment and frustration. If we are genetically simpler than we once thought to be the case, then why can't we more easily manipulate and "improve" our genes? Why can't we master our genes to extend longevity and improve the quality of our lives? Hence the declaration of war against aging and death. Yet this is to make, in secular guise, a previous theological mistake of interpreting death as punishment for the fall. A number of early theologians presumed that humans had been created, like the angels, with an immortal nature. When they sinned their natures were corrupted, thereby allowing death to occur. What this analysis implies, however, is that death is somehow unnatural, and if so, then why can't humans, on their own initiative, restore their natural condition of immortality?

The argument fails to recognize, however, that in the biblical story Adam and Eve were created as mortal beings who would enjoy immortal lives so long as perfect relationships with God and neighbor were maintained. In severing these relationships humans experienced death as mortal creatures.[8] In short, there is nothing *inherently* evil or tragic in a human condition that is finite and mortal; rather, evil and tragedy occur when humans, as finite and mortal creatures, attempt to vanquish death on their own terms. Consequently, attempts at recovering a so-called original perfection that conquers an unnatural death are misguided and futile. This is why regarding aging as a disease that can be treated, and perhaps cured, should at least challenge the assumption that a good destiny is being pursued. Again, there is nothing wrong with medicine using genomics to develop more efficacious treatments. But there is a profound moral difference in medicine hospitably keeping company with the ill and waging a war against aging. As John Passmore has argued, whenever public attention is seized by the prospect of human perfection, however that state might be defined, it is accompanied by increased indifference or intolerance for those judged incapable of achieving the goal.[9]

This sobering observation leads to the second maxim: *medicine should use genomics to strengthen, rather than weaken, the bonds of human association.* Again, the Human Genome Project has disclosed that there is much less genetic variation among humans than many had anticipated. This similarity would not have surprised St. Augustine, who was keen on stressing that all people share the original set of parents, Eve and Adam. He would be offended by the emblem emblazoned on U.S. coins—*e pluribus unum*—for his motto was "out of the one, many." The good bishop of Hippo emphasized this common origin to counter the pagan notion of a natural inequality and hierarchy. Contrary to the Greeks, women, slaves, and barbarians were not naturally inferior to the free men of Athens.[10]

Despite the many commonalities, however, slight genetic variations and expressions can promote strong social and political reactions. Civil communities are already dealing with sharp racial, ethnic, religious, and economic divides, and to what extent the growing knowledge of genomics, especially as applied to healthcare, will ease or exacerbate the ill effects of these divisions remains an open question. My concern is not that a new division between the genetically enhanced and unenhanced will be created. What is more troubling is the prospect that genetic indications will be employed to exclude a growing number of individuals from the moral community. The most obvious example of this tendency is the changing perception of individuals with disabilities.[11] Instead of seeing them as people with special needs, are they not beginning to be perceived as "mistakes" that could have been prevented if only better testing and screening had been available? This is not to suggest that we are on the verge of enacting a new round of draconian eugenic statutes. Rather, in applying genomics and medicine for the humane purpose of preventing suffering, we may be proving Passmore's thesis correct once again by a subtle, but nonetheless pervasive, promotion of indifferent and intolerant attitudes toward people with disabilities or preventable chronic conditions.

For example, I once listened to a doctor on a talk radio program who took a question from a caller who was concerned that he and his wife both carried the recessive genes for cystic fibrosis. They wanted to start a family; should they use PGD? Within a span of less than five minutes, the doctor managed to combine the concepts of "prevention" and "tragedy" within a single sentence on seven occasions. For instance: it would be tragic if the caller did nothing to prevent the birth of a child who would be subjected to a life of suffering. He and his wife should do whatever is necessary to avoid the tragedy of caring for such a child. It would be a tragic waste of expensive medical resources and personnel to treat a condition that could be prevented. Although one might sympathize with the concerns raised by this doctor and caller, should we not also be troubled by the possibility that their brief exchange is symptomatic of a narrowing moral vision? Is it not hard to avoid the conclusion that when certain genetic indications are present, that a judgment has been made that the eventual life would be of such a diminished quality that it would not be worth living, and it would therefore be better to spare the child and parents such a fate?

St. Augustine had much to say about how "monstrosities," a description that admittedly offends late modern sensibilities, should be treated. He insists that regardless of how different they appear to be, and regardless of the tragic circumstances they might suffer, they are nonetheless kin and are to be embraced as such to the fullest extent possible, for they are humans who share a common lineage back to the original parents. St. Augustine's observation remains a salient one, for he urges deliberation on how genomics and its medical applications might be used in ways that enlarge our moral vision in a charitable and hospitable manner, rather than constricting it by becoming fixated on prevention.

The pervading emphasis on preventing the birth of children with disabilities leads to the final maxim: *medicine should use genomics to enrich, rather than to impoverish, intergenerational relationships.* One consequence of the Human Genome Project is that it has revealed both the beauty and the genius of the evolutionary process. Over time it has produced a species called human that is elegantly simple and wondrously complex, an earthly creature little lower than the angels.[12] Moreover, it did this without humans controlling the process. In short, human life might be at its best when it is allowed to unfold over time in a random manner. In this respect, Francis Fukuyama may be right when he warns that extensive genetic manipulation could jeopardize the quality of life that late moderns currently enjoy.[13] Or to phrase the issue more constructively, Hannah Arendt contends that natality should be the overarching moral symbol for shaping the human condition. The birth of a child, the emergence of a new generation, embodies unique and renewing possibilities, and she insists these possibilities are present precisely because offspring are not controlled by their parents. Future generations embody hope because they are not merely projections or replications of their progenitors.[14]

In reflecting on the morality of intergenerational relationships, Jürgen Habermas goes too far in his insistence that using PGD is tantamount to one generation asserting tyrannical control over subsequent ones.[15] Yet he is right to raise the issue that in asserting greater technological control over the beginning of life, such as selecting for and against certain genetic indications or traits, the unconditional relationship between parents and children is being corroded, and that perhaps little by little children are effectively being transformed into artifacts. In this respect, Oliver O'Donovan's insistence that children should be begotten rather than made is instructive. Begetting implies a fundamental equality between parents and children, a giving and receiving of life that binds them together, whereas making entails inequality between the creator and the finished product.[16]

Ironically, by fixating on increasing longevity—both of oneself and of one's offspring—late moderns become more focused on death than life. In warring against aging and death, they deny that the flourishing of life is predicated upon the passing of old generations and the advent of new ones. Life is the emergence of the new and not the prolongation of the old. Again, ironically, in supposedly trying to give their children the best possible start in life, late moderns may actually be limiting their possibilities. The challenge, therefore, is one of embracing a moral vision that promotes the medical application of genomics in ways that do not constrain new possibilities and encourages them as acts of charity and hospitality to future generations.

I reiterate that as a theologian I have no complaint with either the science of human genetics or the medical treatments it is helping to develop. Particularly as a Christian, I celebrate those instances when the lame walk, the blind see, and the infirm are made whole, and whether the source of this healing is miraculous or medical is a matter of indifference, for in either case it is a good gift to be received with gratitude. Yet as a Christian theologian I am also aware of the seemingly infinite capacity humans have for self-deception, and I worry whether this good gift is being used properly. It is not so much the case that late moderns are dedicated to creating a brave new world, but that inadvertently they may be fashioning an uncharitable and inhospitable culture. Hence the need for self-appraisal and critically assessing how new medical treatments are being developed and applied, and the need of properly ordering one's desire so that medicine is being used to care and heal in a right way. Consequently, we need to ask ourselves, and each other, frequently: what purposes are improved diagnostic, therapeutic, preventive, and enhancement techniques serving, and, more importantly, how should they be used?

4

Persons, Neighbors, and Embryos

Some Ethical Reflections on Human Cloning and Stem Cell Research

The prospect of human cloning and embryonic stem cell research is a highly divisive issue, and the acrimonious debates over its morality and legality often generate more heat than light. This is due, in part, to the poisonous political environment bequeathed by *Roe v. Wade*. In the United States, pondering the moral and legal status of prenatal life is to immediately send a rallying cry to the pro-life and pro-choice camps to mobilize their respective armies. In reaction to cloning and embryonic stem cell research, old slogans, both in support and in opposition, are dusted off and invoked, although their relevance for this particular debate is often far from clear.

A more civil form of public discourse needs to be fashioned on this issue, one in which citizens engage each other as reasonable people of good will who disagree, often profoundly, over how the common good should be pursued, rather than waging a rhetorical Armageddon. Moreover, such discourse is needed, because what is at stake is important if not crucial. Whether, as a civil community, Americans choose to either pursue or refrain from cloning and embryonic stem cell research, the costs will be high, and they will be moral and spiritual as well as economic and political. Clear-headed thinking and honest debate are required to determine what these costs might be, and whether or not the price is worth paying.

Consequently, whenever I think about the prospect of human cloning and embryonic stem cell research, I try to keep in mind the Spanish proverb that was mentioned in a previous chapter: "Take what you want, said God—take it and pay for it."[1] This sobering adage applies to both individuals and communities. If we choose to proceed, then we must be prepared to offer good reasons for willfully destroying thousands of embryos, and if we choose not to proceed, then we must also give reasons why the suffering of individuals, which perhaps could have been treated by new therapies, is justified. In other words, whatever decision we eventually make will be accompanied by troubling consequences.

Assessing these costs is not an easy task, for there is no common starting point to begin deliberating, no consensus regarding what the moral status of the human embryo is or should be. For late moderns, that status is highly fluid and assigned, rather than static and given. An embryo in a womb and an embryo in a laboratory, for instance, are viewed and valued differently, respectively, by an expectant couple and a research scientist. What is at stake is whether they are viewing the same thing but valuing it differently, or whether their values shape entirely disparate viewpoints. This is why clarity is needed regarding what an embryo is, how various definitions conflict, and what contending moral convictions shape these conflicting definitions. This is a daunting task, for it requires extensive and expansive deliberation and debate, yet it is worth pursuing if a more civil form of public discourse is to be fashioned, and I hope this chapter will make a modest contribution to this effort.

Before proceeding, however, I must make three disclaimers: first, for the purpose of this inquiry, "cloning" refers to what is commonly called therapeutic cloning. The same technology can admittedly be used for reproductive purposes, but the issue at stake is complicated enough, so I am keeping the possibility of human reproductive cloning off the table. Yet cloning cannot be ignored altogether, for it will be required if medical applications of embryonic stem cell research are to be efficacious. Second, my perspective is that of a Christian theologian, for which I make no apology. The issues at stake are certainly medical, ethical, political, and philosophical, but they are also inescapably religious. To deny or stifle religious voices in pondering the ethics of cloning and embryonic stem cell research would be to pursue an incomplete and dishonest public debate.

Finally, my reservations regarding cloning and embryonic stem cell research are the result of ambivalence rather than any certitude regarding the moral status of the human embryo. It is not an ambivalence based on indifference, however, but a deep respect for the potential costs at stake. Yet I know that I do not know enough to assess what these costs might be, and I therefore need the company of other viewpoints and expertise. In short, I hope this chapter proves to be, for the reader, a conversation starter instead of a stopper. In initiating this conversation, I first examine the philosophical principle of *personhood* and argue that it does not offer a good starting point for civil discourse. I then contend that the alternative concept of embryo as *neighbor* offers a more promising starting point. I conclude by exploring what difference this shift from person to neighbor might make in respect to specific moral and public policy *proposals*.

Persons

Is the human embryo a person? Most disputes over the moral status of the embryo tend to focus on this question. Three prevalent answers can be summarized briefly. One answer is that all embryos are persons in virtue of their classification as members of the human species. From the moment egg and sperm are joined to form a new living creature to the moment that creature dies, it should be afforded all the respect and protection that is due any other living human being. To do less is to assault an inherent human dignity. To treat some humans, such as embryos, as nonpersons is to introduce a subjective and disturbing distinction, one easily lending itself to widespread moral abuse. Although extracting stem cells from embryos may promote great medical advances, it does not justify their willful deaths.

A second answer is that embryos are not persons, because that designation requires certain qualitative characteristics beyond mere

79

membership in the human species. A person, for instance, is conscious and self-aware. More importantly, persons, unlike embryos, have an interest in how they should be treated. In this respect, they are more akin to tissue than persons; an embryo, like tissue, is living but is not alive. Medicine is therefore justified in using embryos in much the same way it uses tissue or organs to treat ill persons. The real affront against human dignity is to treat embryos as if they are the same as persons, for it reduces human life to the level of mere biology, rather than emphasizing the higher capacity for autobiography.

A third answer is that human embryos are potential persons. Invoking a developmental understanding of personhood, this answer seeks to position itself as a centrist alternative to the previous two stances. The principal claim is that personhood is a status that is gradually acquired over time. Contrary to the first answer, embryos should not be afforded full moral regard and protection, because they are not yet fully persons. Contrary to the second answer, however, this does not entitle scientists and physicians to treat them merely as tissue, since they have the potential to become persons. The task is to determine, albeit imprecisely, at what developmental point prenatal life should be granted full moral regard and protection, and what type of procedures and regulations should be in place to exhibit respect prior to achieving that threshold.

What these differing answers demonstrate is that it is unlikely that any consensus regarding the moral status of the embryo based on the presence or absence of personhood will soon emerge. Rather, to pursue a public debate on the ethics of cloning and embryonic stem cell research fixated on the question of personhood will only widen existing political, moral, and religious divisions, deep chasms already exposed in the ongoing battles over abortion, assisted suicide, and euthanasia. Moreover, even in the unlikely event that a consensus would emerge around one of these three answers, it would provide neither a sufficient framework for determining the moral status of the human embryo nor adequate ethical guidance regarding the prospect of cloning and embryonic stem cell research.

In the first instance, preserving an inherent human dignity would presumably entail a total prohibition of cloning and embryonic stem cell research. If embryos are persons, this research must be banned, since they cannot freely consent to participate. This is a peculiar claim, however, for the concept of personhood invoked places a heavy emphasis on individual autonomy, which is derived from liberal democratic principles. It is thereby difficult to see how the resulting dignity is inherent rather than assigned as a cultural construct.

Moreover, if the personhood of embryos were accepted in principle, then it would call into question many other practices, such as reproductive technologies employing surplus embryos, preimplantation genetic diagnosis, abortion, assisted suicide, most forms of euthanasia, and more expansively, capital punishment, and lethal police and military force. What is not clear in each of these instances is whose dignity is assaulted or endangered. In the case of capital punishment, for example, is it the criminal or the executioner who is subjected to an indignity or performing an undignified act? This is a matter of interpretation as witnessed by the crosses and crucifixes hanging in Christian churches. In respect to cloning and embryonic stem cell research, it is not clear whose dignity is imperiled: the embryo's because it is destroyed, or the researcher's because she is the destroyer? This again is a matter of interpretation. Simply asserting the personhood of embryos does not really reveal much about human dignity, and therefore it cannot serve as an objective or universal guiding principle for establishing the moral status of the embryo, much less the ethical conduct of research.

The second response that embryos are not persons is equally problematic. To assert that the moral community is populated by persons rather than human beings is troubling, for there are no precise criteria to determine when one is admitted (or has exited) this realm of full moral regard and protection. At what point does living tissue become a living person? Fourteen days after conception? Six months of gestation? Birth? One year following birth? Moreover, some individuals, because of severe disabilities, may never become persons, while many others, due to illness or injury, may cease to be persons. Yet when being merely human no longer counts—or at least is not the overriding consideration—then the realm of moral regard is subjected to periodic expansion and contraction. As with appealing to a mythical "inherent dignity," personhood is also a social construct, and its criteria can be redefined in line with changing interests and values; the rules governing who is in and who is out of the personhood club can be amended as needed. This does not imply any sinister motives regarding the establishment and amendment of these rules. More often than not, nonpersons are not treated in a cavalier manner. Yet it must not be forgotten that with the possibility of changing political fortunes and social mores, the category of nonpersons could be greatly expanded, as witnessed by the atrocities committed by the totalitarian regimes of the twentieth century.

Moreover, it is not clear why personhood is presumably the sole criterion for extending full moral regard and protection. In the current debate over cloning and embryonic stem cell research, there is often an underlying assumption that if embryos are not persons, then it is permissible to do anything one may want with them. Hence, the fierce political battles waged at this philosophical Rubicon as reflected in many of the reports submitted by the President's Council on Bioethics. It is not apparent, however, why moral regard cannot or should not be extended to so-called nonpersons. It could be argued, for instance, that nonpersons should be afforded even greater regard and protection than persons, given their weakness and vulnerability.

The third option of a developmental understanding of personhood has much to commend. It recognizes that there is no precise point where living tissue becomes a living person, yet it rejects the presumption that one may therefore do anything one may want with prenatal life. Rather, embryos should be respected as potential persons, as demonstrated through moral and legal limits regarding their treatment. Particularly in regard to embryonic research, this respect is exhibited through regulatory procedures and protocols as seen in the United Kingdom's fourteen-day limit, and restrictive licensing.

The strength of this stance, however, is also its weakness. In admitting that there is no precise or objective threshold where personhood is reached, whatever point that is set will be arbitrary and fluid. Consequently, it can, at best, offer only a compromise solution in respect to cloning and embryonic stem cell research that is bound to disappoint the first two stances (embryos as persons, and embryos as nonpersons), promoting ongoing acrimony. Moreover, it does not establish *the* moral status of the embryo, for such a status is still largely determined by particular contexts. Setting a fourteen-day research limit, for instance, has no applicability to laws governing abortion in the United Kingdom. Moreover, it is, at best, ambiguous how subjecting embryos to research protocols ending inevitably in their destruction is demonstrating a respect for potential persons.

In short, revisiting the seemingly endless debate over whether or not an embryo is a person will not resolve disputes over the morality of human cloning and embryonic stem cell research. It is unlikely that a consensus will be reached, and even if some agreement emerges, it is doubtful that any obvious policy solution would be forthcoming. If personhood is not a good starting point for civil discourse and debate, is there a more promising alternative?

Neighbors

Thinking about embryos as neighbors *might* offer such an alternative. What exactly is a neighbor? Following Karl Barth, neighbors cannot be contemplated as abstractions but are encountered through various relationships.[2] There are neighbors near and far, and neighbors we know and neighbors we have never met. We have neighbors who are our friends, and neighbors who are our enemies, neighbors who are persons, and neighbors who are not persons. Most importantly, when encountering unfamiliar neighbors we should presume that we share a bond by the fact that we both exist, however qualitatively different that existence might be.

Regarding embryos as neighbors may admittedly appear too fanciful to be of much practical use. We cannot really treat embryos as neighbors, because we cannot interact or form relationships with them. To regard an embryo as a neighbor requires an imaginative leap that most reasonable people are unwilling to take. Being a neighbor, however, does not always require reciprocity or even interaction. We are capable of protecting nameless and vulnerable neighbors, even assisting some we never meet or directly encounter as demonstrated by impersonal acts of kindness or generosity. We may donate money or items, for instance, in response to disasters that occur in foreign and faraway places. That regarding embryos as neighbors is an imaginative leap should not prevent us from undertaking the intellectual challenge to do so. Previous generations must have felt challenged in their initial attempts to include more fully, for example, women, children, and slaves in their moral vision, yet most today would judge their efforts to be highly worthwhile. Moreover, at a time when serious proposals are being issued that urge the ethical treatment of animals within an expanded sphere of friendship,[3] it is not all that fanciful to regard human embryos within a realm of neighborliness. If we can entertain the possibility of treating animals as friends, is it an unimaginable stretch to regard embryos as neighbors?

Assuming that such a stretch is possible, what moral difference does it make to regard the human embryo as a neighbor instead of a person, potential person, or nonperson? The difference is twofold. First, the foundation of moral regard is not predicated on the presence or absence of personhood. A fellow human being is, by definition, a neighbor, but this does not mean that all neighbors should be regarded equally simply because they are human. Parents, for example, should regard their offspring more highly than other children. But this higher regard does not mean they should have no regard whatsoever for other children because they are not their offspring. If my daughter is cold, I do not have the right to take a coat away from another girl, because she is, so to speak, a non-daughter. Rather, I must exercise my parental duties within the moral constraints of how I should treat other children as my neighbors.

Second, the different contexts in which neighbors are encountered provide some important clues on how they should be treated. For instance, we hold neighbors who are friends in higher regard than neighbors who are enemies. We would rightfully defend our friends if attacked by an enemy, and under certain circumstances we might be justified in using lethal force. Protecting our friends, however, does not mean that we may treat enemies without any moral regard, because they are non-friends. Defending my neighbors who are my friends does not give me the right to exterminate or decimate the homeland of my neighbors who are my enemies. Most importantly, the love for neighbor in this context is expressed both in defending friends *and* in the temperate use of lethal force against enemies. Exhibiting a proper love for neighbors who are friends may, regrettably, entail killing, though not slaughtering, neighbors who are enemies. Moreover, it is important to emphasize that in fulfilling this moral duty, young women and men may be asked, and at times required (through conscription), to place their lives in danger or even sacrifice themselves in providing such protection.

We may also say that medicine is a way of expressing the love of neighbor. The civil community treats and prevents disease and disability to exhibit care and concern for its citizens and residents. Medicine is an important office and practice to maintain the bonds of fellowship between healthy and ill neighbors. Indeed, it would be immoral to perceive illness or disability as a condition that disqualified an individual from the civil community. Consequently, the commitment to maintaining, and even strengthening, this social bond is exhibited through the private and public funding of healthcare and research facilities. It is within the context of this social bond that moral deliberation on the tasks and limits of medicine should be undertaken.

There are some who contend that this bond can be strengthened by developing more efficacious therapies based on embryonic stem cell research. A wide range of debilitating and deadly diseases can, perhaps, in the future be cured, or at least greatly ameliorated, *if* this research is pursued aggressively. This is a highly contentious and divisive proposal, and if the civil community chooses not to pursue this research, then it is also obligated to offer a morally coherent reason why a need to protect embryos trumps the need for developing more effective medical treatments. After all, if young women and men can be expected or required to sacrifice their lives for the sake of protecting their civil neighbors, is the prospect of sacrificing embryos really all that appalling?

Before that question can be addressed, however, some larger ramifications need to be considered. As mentioned above, the contexts in which neighbors are encountered provide some important clues on how they should be regarded and treated. We are now endeavoring to think about the ethical treatment of embryos within a novel context or set of circumstances. Unlike previous generations, embryos may now be created for the *sole* purpose of conducting scientific research. It is important that the civil community comes to terms with the sheer novelty of this capability, for it requires stripping away the procreative and familial contexts in which previous generations thought about and performed their responsibilities in relation to prenatal life. Yet in stripping away these procreative and familial contexts, is not the human embryo also being extracted out from the very social and moral settings in which its meaning and worth are discerned? If we entertain the possibility that an embryo may be created without any intention of implanting it in a womb, what exactly is this "object" or "artifact" that we behold and whose fate we contemplate?

This novel context may produce some subtle, but nevertheless troubling, consequences. The philosophers Hannah Arendt and Hans Jonas, for instance, spent a great deal of time pondering the social and moral significance of natality and mortality.[4] Birth and death are, of course, definitive features of human life, but they also represent far more moral and political significance. Following Arendt and Jonas, intergenerational relationships are the most significant features in forming the moral character and aspirations of the civil community. Natality signifies not only hope for the survival of the community, but also the possibility of a better future. The birth of each child, therefore, embodies both this hope and possibility, for a new life is not only the result of biological reproduction, but also an act of social and political reproduction. In this respect, medicine traditionally not only treated the ill health of individuals but also promoted a healthy relationship between generations.

If natality is to carry this heavy symbolic weight, then we must also come to terms with the necessity of mortality. It is in consenting to our eventual and inevitable deaths that we are enabled to give more freely of ourselves to the generations succeeding us, and this self-giving serves to promote altruism, while checking narcissistic tendencies. Consequently, separating the human embryo from a procreative and familial context is bound to have larger moral, social, and political implications, for attention is now directed toward preserving the present generation rather than its successor. In this respect, in helping patients come to terms with their inherent mortality, medicine also contributes to the welfare of future generations.

The concern at stake is that we may have already effectively shifted away from emphasizing natality to avoiding or mitigating mortality. Have we not already, to a considerable degree, redirected our attention, as expressed through the development of new medical treatments, away from intergenerational relationships to maximizing individual survival and personal longevity? When human cloning and embryonic stem cell research are placed within the advent of a much more ambitious enterprise called "regenerative medicine,"[5] it appears that a medical war against aging and death has already been initiated. Presumably, embryonic stem cells offer the prospect of developing some highly promising weapons in this struggle.

As has been emphasized in previous chapters, there is nothing inherently wrong in living longer and healthier lives, and medicine should be celebrated as a good gift in achieving this worthwhile goal. Yet some hard issues must be faced if aging is regarded as a disease that presumably can be treated and perhaps cured. How do we fight aging and cure mortality? What would victory mean, and what would be the cost? Any answer may require a subtle but significant change in moral vision, one in which the embryo is no longer viewed as a symbol of hope and possibility, but as a biological and medical commodity to be consumed. Would such a change in perspective have a corrosive and coarsening effect of our moral sensibilities over time? My discomfort with the prospect of human cloning and embryonic stem cell research, in the simplest terms, is not only the prospect of destroying embryos, but the impact this will have on those willing their destruction for the sake of their own survival and increased longevity.

It may be countered that my discomfort is misplaced. The corrosive and coarsening consequences I fear are not inevitable, for my concern is symbolic, not substantive. The civil community can be self-critical and vigilant to ensure that the scope of this research remains narrowly regulated, and does not lead to unwanted or unwarranted applications. The civil community may perhaps be successful in its self-regulation, but symbols *do* form the moral imagination, and acts originating in the imagination have substantive consequences. The formative influence of symbols remains, more often than not, hidden and unacknowledged, rather than obvious and admitted. For over two centuries, for example, the American civil community has been dedicated to the symbols of life, liberty, and the pursuit of happiness, yet irrational prejudice and discrimination continue, despite self-critical vigilance to corrupt these noble sentiments. There is simply no way of knowing in advance if extracting embryonic stem cells will enlarge or restrict the breadth of a community's moral vision, and that is a risk that needs to be acknowledged deliberately and realistically.

Admittedly, shifting the imagery from the embryo as person, nonperson, or potential person to the embryo as neighbor does not help us avoid an equally unhappy dilemma. On the one hand, if we choose to use embryos to improve healthcare for various neighbors, then we also run the risk of moral corrosion or decline. Will this decision bequeath to future generations clarity of moral vision, or moral myopia? On the other hand, if we believe this risk is too great, then we condemn a number of ill neighbors to pain and suffering that might otherwise be cured or effectively treated. Will this decision bequeath to future generations strength of character, or moral cowardice in the face of unknown fears? I frankly admit that I have no answer, at least no certain answer, to this dilemma.

Proposals

Since I have no answer to offer, this chapter concludes with four proposals, based more on my ignorance than expertise. The first proposal is directed toward physicians and research scientists: what would be lost if an international moratorium on embryonic stem cell research was to be enacted, while at the same time promoting private and public funding investigating alternative sources? Is it feasible to determine the range of treatments that could be developed with these alternative sources, exhausting their potential before returning to the issue of embryonic stem cells? Would this approach provide a sufficient body of scientific information both for developing potentially effective therapies, and for informing subsequent public discourse and policy guidelines? Recent experiments involving somatic cell reprogramming do not negate the need for this proposed moratorium. It is too early to know if this procedure is capable of developing efficacious therapies. Additional experiments with embryos may also be needed for establishing benchmarks that measure the potency and potential efficacy of reprogrammed stem cells. If so, it remains problematic if embryos should be destroyed in setting benchmarks that in turn might prevent the destruction of embryos in the future. More broadly, if somatic cell reprogramming proves effective, a host of moral, social, and political issues still need to be addressed. A "morally acceptable" source of stem cells, for example, may simply exacerbate the intergenerational concerns noted above.

The second proposal is directed toward policy makers and the general public: if it is determined that human cloning and embryonic stem cell research should be permitted, either following or in the absence of a research moratorium, what laws and regulations need to be enacted to prevent the moral corrosion I fear, assuming that this is a legitimate public concern? If creating and cloning human embryos to extract their stem cells is deemed justified, then what realistic steps should be taken to ensure that they are treated as neighbors, and are not reduced to biological raw material to be exploited in manufacturing and consuming medical commodities?

The third proposal is directed specifically toward Christians: they should, as citizens, participate in the public debates on embryonic stem cell research, but it must be informed participation. It is incumbent upon Christians to acquaint themselves with the science, and the true potential and limits of medical applications. In addition, the temptation to impugn the motives of scientists and biotechnology firms conducting embryonic stem cell research and developing various therapies should be resisted. To simply presume that those promoting embryonic stem cell research are motivated by greed or other self-interested values is neither charitable nor factual. Again, it is incumbent upon Christians to familiarize themselves with the economic incentives, risks, and constraints that are inherent to conducting such research, and developing and distributing medical treatments.

The fourth proposal is again directed toward Christians: although they will use a "second language" in participating in civil debate on human cloning and embryonic stem cell research, their discourse must nonetheless remain grounded in the gospel. Care should be taken that what is translated into public parlance does not distort core theological convictions that have formed a moral vision shaped by scripture, prayer, worship, and the sacraments. Their interest in this debate, for instance, is not fixated on establishing healthcare as a right or entitlement, but on the gift of healing and care given and received among neighbors. Like their ancestors in the faith, late modern Christians rejoice when those who are not well are made well. In short, it is through their participation in civil debate and governance that Christians also bear witness to and embody their obedient discipleship of the Lord Jesus Christ, and in doing so help to partially fulfill their calling to evangelize the world in his name.

5

Extending Human Life

To What End?

The burgeoning field of regenerative medicine is poised to transform healthcare. Advances in genetics, stem cell research, and cloning suggest that late moderns may be on the brink of enjoying a golden age of medical care, culminating in greatly extended longevity. These advances, however, are accompanied by a number of troubling and divisive religious, moral, and political issues. Although careful analyses are being devoted to resolving a wide range of discrete problems, the issue of toward what larger end regenerative medicine is headed has received inadequate attention. How are the rapid and anticipated developments in the technologies of regenerative medicine shaping religious, moral, and political visions of the future? Particularly in respect to extended longevity, how much longer should future generations expect to live? So long as an acceptable quality is maintained, the answer is presumably that one's life cannot be too long. Yet in the absence of an outside limit, does this not suggest that the advent of regenerative medicine may mark the initial skirmish in a war against aging, if not death itself? If so, what would victory mean, and what would be the cost? In this chapter I address these questions through the following four-part inquiry: 1) I summarize the most prominent technological developments in regenerative medicine to date and their accompanying ethical issues; 2) I analyze selected implications of treating aging as a disease; 3) I examine four responses to the prospect of humans aspiring to become posthuman; and 4) I critically assess these responses in light of their connotations for medicine and bioethics.

Revolutionizing Medicine

Genetics is the basic science underlying regenerative medicine. Recombinant DNA technology, for instance, is currently used to produce human-protein drugs to treat diabetes and promote the formation of red blood cells. New protein drugs are also being developed to treat a greater range of diseases. It is anticipated that genes can be used to stimulate the growth of new tissue and create antibodies. These antibodies in turn may be used either to suppress or to enhance the immune system to treat such diseases as rheumatoid arthritis and various cancers. The principal advantage of this approach is that unlike chemically based drugs that merely support failing or damaged organs or tissue, regenerative medicine cures disease and repairs the damage while having less toxic side effects.

Cellular biology also plays a major role in regenerative medicine. Human cells are already employed in manufacturing artificial skin and growing blood vessels. Stem cells offer even more promising treatments. It is anticipated that adult stem cells can be harvested, cultured and reinserted to heal damaged or worn-out tissue, bones, nerves, and organs, producing highly prized therapies for those suffering brain and spinal injures, and more generally aging populations. Adult stem cells, however, often prove difficult to locate and activate, and may be ineffective in treating a number of diseases and injuries because of their limited flexibility. Alternatively, embryonic stem cells may provide a resource that is easier to obtain, and their plasticity offers potentially greater therapeutic benefit. A major hurdle to be overcome is that inserting adult or embryonic stem cells into a host that is not genetically matched will trigger an immune reaction. One way to overcome this difficulty is to clone embryos that are created from the patient's cell sample.

Prosthetics is another instrument in regenerative medicine's tool chest. Fabricated hip joints, heart valves, blood vessels, and cochleas are now routinely employed. Recent experiments suggest the feasibility of curing blindness with artificial retinas and overcoming paralysis with neural implants. More speculatively, nanotechnology holds the promise of continuous diagnostic monitoring, augmenting immune systems, and tissue and organ repair without invasive surgery. Neural implants may someday amplify memory and cognitive abilities, as well as provide a direct connection with external computer networks.[1]

The benefits of regenerative medicine are obvious. Greater diagnostic precision offers early and more effective medical interventions. Exploring the intricacies of the map produced by the Human Genome Project and nearly ubiquitous monitoring will allow medicine to react to the early onset of debilitating and life-threatening diseases. More effective therapies improve the quality of many patients' lives. Diseased or damaged organs, for instance, will be repaired or replaced completely, thereby restoring a patient's health entirely. Regenerative medicine prevents illness and disability more effectively. Genetically or prosthetically enhanced immune systems will replace cumbersome inoculations. In addition, physical and cognitive performance can be enhanced. Various therapies will be employed to augment a variety of normal functions. Drugs, for example, might be used to improve memory or optical implants be employed to provide telescopic or night vision. In short, the singular benefit of regenerative medicine is that many individuals will live longer and healthier lives.

These benefits, however, are accompanied by a number of controversies. These disputes are well known, and a few examples are noted to plot out the scope of the issues at stake. As suggested in the previous chapter, will embryonic stem cell research and therapeutic cloning lead to a callous disregard and commodification of human life at its most vulnerable stage? Or to the contrary, are attempts at restricting or prohibiting their rapid development callously condemning countless individuals to needless suffering? Will the benefits of regenerative medicine be evenly distributed, or will they be available only to the wealthy? More broadly, what will be the social, economic, and political ramifications of societies populated by genetically and prosthetically enhanced individuals of varying levels? Does this prospect call for greater or lesser regulation of the research underlying regenerative medicine? Is regenerative medicine transforming healthcare into an institution that is increasingly divorced from its antecedents in providing care rather than cure?

These are admittedly sweeping questions that incorporate a number of discrete issues that are vexing and contentious in their own right. For example: what are the contending religious, moral, and ideological convictions that are seeking to shape public discourse on embryonic stem cell research and therapeutic cloning? How does this discourse in turn inform ethical codes of conduct, laws, public policies, and funding of scientific research? As noted above, these discrete issues require detailed analysis. Such meticulous inquiries, however, are themselves shaped by larger religious, moral, and ideological convictions. Toward what end are current and anticipated developments in regenerative medicine directing its patients? And how do we assess whether this end is good or desirable? The remainder of this chapter takes a step back to catch a glimpse of the horizon toward which regenerative medicine is headed.

Waging War against Death

If the principal benefit of regenerative medicine is improved health, then presumably its beneficiaries will also live longer lives. The development of superior diagnostic, therapeutic, preventive, and enhancement techniques is bound to raise the statistical norm for average life expectancy. Yet if three-score-and-ten has become obsolete, what measure should replace it—100, 150, 500 years, or more? At present, science cannot offer any definitive answer to what the outside limit might be. If embryonic stem cells, for instance, prove to be as potent and pliable as hoped, then the possibility of infinite tissue and organ rejuvenation cannot be ruled out. Moreover, if attempts at cellular manipulation encounter stubborn obstacles, ever more sophisticated prosthetics can be developed to achieve similar results.

The prospect of living longer does not suggest that regenerative medicine is merely a high-tech version of Ponce de Leon's vain quest for youthful immortality. Yet extended longevity has certainly been a factor in creating public interest and investment in the fledging biotechnology industry. The names of such companies as Geron and Osiris, and discoveries of "immortality" and "fountain of youth" genes, have captured the attention of elderly venture capitalists and aging baby boomers.[2] Such hyperbole is bound to skew and disappoint public expectations, but there is nonetheless a growing perception, in both the industrial and medical literature, that aging is akin to a disease that can be treated. In the absence of any known outside limit, however, what constitutes effective treatment? Without a given limit it would appear that regenerative medicine is the first step in an endless struggle against growing old. If medical resources become increasingly developed and deployed for this purpose, however, does it not raise a rather awkward question: is aging a disease that can be cured? This question helps us to get at the heart of the matter, because the chief benefit of regenerative medicine is its ability to cure rather than merely treat disease or injury. It is through rejuvenating the functions of tissue and organs that longevity is extended. Consequently, to cure aging is not to contend against the passage of time, but against the accompanying cellular degeneration and resulting morbidity.

If aging is regarded as a disease to be cured, however, does this not suggest that the advent of regenerative medicine also signals a declaration of war against the old enemy, death? Presumably the answer must be yes, for death is the end result of degeneration and morbidity. Yet what would victory against this old foe mean, and what would be the cost? Total victory would be immortality, and if this ambitious goal proves elusive, greatly expanded longevity would represent a partial but nonetheless significant triumph. The cost of winning this war would be the radical transformation of medicine as a practice *and* its patients. To wage war against death requires that medicine forsake its traditional emphasis on caring in favor of curing.[3] The chief medical practice would no longer be providing care and comfort to patients suffering the ravages of illness and deteriorating bodies, but to eliminate the organic sources of their suffering. The role of medicine would not be one of assisting patients to come to terms with their mortal state, but to enable them to vanquish mortality or at least keep degeneration and morbidity at bay for a more extensive period of time. Moreover, if an effective war against death is to be waged, then medicine must in turn transform its patients. The move from care to cure entails that the line separating therapy and enhancement be blurred if not erased. This is particularly the case at the cellular level, in which a combination of bio- and nanotechnologies is deployed to overcome the Hayflick limit,[4] effectively reengineering the patient. Consequently, the patient is simultaneously the beneficiary and artifact of such transformative medicine. Medicine is no longer dedicated to relieving the human condition but is radically changing it.

If regenerative medicine is the first step in curing aging and an act of war against death, then a provocative issue is forced upon us, namely, should humans use their technology to become something other than human? It would seem that some such aspiration is at play if the goal is to use technology to overcome or extend the mortal limits that evolution has programmed into the human biology. Yet if these limits are overcome or greatly extended, then mortality is no longer a definitive feature of human life. Yet in the absence of this definitive feature, what are humans aspiring to become as artifacts of their own engineering? Or to pose the question more starkly: should humans aspire to become posthuman?

Should We Become Posthuman?

The purpose for posing this question is neither to implicate regenerative medicine in some far-fetched conspiracy to create a more grotesque brave new world than that imagined by Huxley nor to associate it with fanciful attempts of elevating the cyborg to iconic status.[5] Rather, the intent is to initiate reflection on the possible future direction that humankind may be heading in taking the initial step of regenerative medicine, and that such imaginative reflection might in turn inform moral and political deliberation on current research priorities. In short, to ponder the prospect of a posthuman future is to reflect on how best to ensure that well-intended efforts to improve the functions of the human body do not inadvertently create beings we would prefer not to become. To ask the question of the future is to place a mirror before the present. To capture some of the reflected images, four possible answers to the question posed above are examined below:

- An unqualified *"yes"* (transhumanists)
- An ambiguous "yes" (N. Katherine Hayles)
- A muted "no" (Francis Fukuyama)
- A resounding *"no"* (Leon Kass)

An unqualified *"yes" (the transhumanists)*

Transhumanists respond with an unqualified "yes" to this question. This loosely knit and ill-defined movement is dedicated to transforming individuals, if not the human species, into posthumans.[6] This goal will be achieved initially by extending longevity through improved diets, and healthcare employing regenerative medical techniques.[7] More expansively, humans will gradually merge with their technology through the application of sophisticated prosthetics, employing anticipated developments in nanotechnology, artificial intelligence, and robotics. This process of technological transformation will culminate in uploading the information constituting one's personality into a computer and downloading it into various media, thereby enabling virtual immortality.[8]

There are two principal reasons why transhumanists aspire to become posthuman. First, pursuing this goal will improve the quality of life for many individuals. For transhumanists, personal identity is defined almost exclusively in terms of subjective experience and cognitive abilities. Admittedly, the human body serves as the means of constructing one's identity through its various senses, but it also imposes severe limitations on individuals, given their limited sensual scope and short life spans. Consequently, transhumanists welcome regenerative medicine as an important tool in enhancing the quality of human life, because it will lead to the "radical extension of human health-span, eradication of disease, elimination of unnecessary suffering, and augmentation of intellectual, physical, and emotional capacities."[9] It is not surprising that transhumanists are among the most vocal proponents of embryonic stem cell research and therapeutic cloning.

Second, humans must use their reason to direct the future course of evolution if they are to flourish as a species. To date, biological evolution has conspired against humans in realizing their full potential, particularly in respect to mortality. In response to this cruel fate, various technologies should be developed as quickly as possible to fulfill this potential. As Nick Bostrom has written: "Transhumanists view human nature as a work-in-progress, a half-baked beginning that we can learn to remold in desirable ways. Current humanity need not be the endpoint of evolution."[10] The problem is that evolution does not allow sufficient "baking time" for humans to maximize their latent potential. It is only through the development of sophisticated prosthetics in tandem with regenerative medical techniques that humans will be able to transform themselves into the superior posthuman creatures they have the potential to become. Contemporary regenerative medicine is a cautious first step in the transformation of *Homo sapiens* into technosapiens.

It is unfair to imply that scientific, medical, and industrial leaders in the field of regenerative medicine are driven by a transhumanist agenda, yet transhumanists nonetheless welcome and champion their work as a means of achieving their more ambitious goals. Pursuing a posthuman future is an urgent task, for failing to do so consigns humans to at best greatly diminished lives, and at worse extinction as a species.[11]

An ambiguous "yes" (N. Katherine Hayles)

N. Katherine Hayles offers an ambiguous reply to the question of whether or not humans should aspire to become posthuman. She agrees that the future is inevitably a posthuman one, for human destiny is inexorably linked with science and technology.[12] Unlike the transhumanists, however, Hayles does not assume a utopian destiny. Rather, she fears that a combination of modern humanistic anthropology and technoscience will prove deadly.[13] A late liberal understanding of individual autonomy is incompatible with the underlying premises of the envisioned technologies, because the former assumes that personhood is delineated in terms of embodied boundaries that should not be violated, while the latter is dedicated to erasing those very borders. The end result is that persons are reduced to little more than assertive wills expressed through various biological and silicon-based prosthetics. Consequently, any attempt to reify individual or corporate identities in terms of virtual immortality is a recipe for unmitigated disaster, because humans disappear within their technology rather than using it to transform themselves.

Alternatively, Hayles wants to create a posthuman that "celebrates finitude as a condition of human being," and this condition is in turn a prerequisite for "our continued survival."[14] Significantly, Hayles shares with her transhumanist interlocutors the assumption that the overriding issue at stake is survival, and that individual and corporate identities are socially constructed rather than imposed by nature, but she disagrees on the best strategy to be undertaken in light of this assumption. The objective should not be to obtain the virtual immortality of a disembodied will, but to construct embodied and finite persons. The principle of finitude presumably places limits on the extent to which humans should employ technology in transforming themselves. It is important to note, however, that Hayles does not specify what these limits should entail, because she is unwilling to make any normative claims about the human body per se. In many respects she celebrates the ability to transgress the borders dividing nature from artifice, because this border has historically been used by the strong to oppress and dominate the weak. But she wants to render these boundaries more pliable and tenuous to liberate oppressed groups and individuals, instead of erasing them altogether, resulting in an equally oppressive condition. The posthuman world should be populated by persons who have constructed their own embodied identities as opposed to disembodied wills that continue a quest to dominate finitude itself. Despite Hayles's unease with the liberal, humanistic, and thereby destructive anthropology reflected (yet also distorted) in many posthuman visions of the future, she is cautiously optimistic that one can be constructed "that will be conducive to the long-range survival of humans."[15]

Hayles does not mention regenerative medicine directly; there is nothing in her account that would either endorse or condemn its various therapies and enhancements. The issue at stake for her is not the transformative power of revolutionary medical technologies, but how these tools are used in constructing an inevitable posthuman future. Yet in refusing to make any normative claims about the limits of finitude, she offers few clues about how these tools should be used for constructive rather than destructive purposes.

A muted "no" (Francis Fukuyama)

For Francis Fukuyama the task at hand is not to construct the future, but to preserve human dignity in whatever future lies ahead. Contrary to Hayles, the challenge is not to avoid the toxic joining of liberal humanism with technoscience, but to prevent biotechnology from undermining the foundation of human nature upon which liberal democracy rests. Most importantly, democracy is the only reliable option available for resisting the kind of tyranny Hayles fears.[16] Fukuyama worries that regenerative medicine represents the first step in engineering humans toward an inhumane future. Augmenting the performance of the human body means that human nature is also being transformed, and he believes that a strong philosophical argument can be offered against this transformation. The gist of his argument may be captured by summarizing two substantive claims. First, any meaningful discourse on human rights must be grounded in human nature, which is defined as "the sum of the behavior and characteristics that are typical of the human species, arising from genetic rather than environmental factors."[17] Individuals, civil societies, and political structures are not created ex nihilo, but are derived from innate behavioral characteristics. The instinct for parental care and affection, for example, helps to account for the institutions of marriage and family that pervade nearly every culture. Moreover, a natural moral sense has evolved over time, as demonstrated in a range of emotive responses that is "species-typical."[18]

The second substantive claim is that dignity is not an abstract concept or free-floating category, but a natural quality derived from a genetic endowment that is uniquely human. It is an endowment promoting emergent rather than reductive forms of behavior among individuals and groups, and any attempt to separate the parts from the whole would result in disfiguring the distinctly *human* nature that has been bequeathed by natural selection. Altering genes, albeit for genuinely therapeutic reasons, is nonetheless also altering human nature. Tinkering with this uniquely human genetic endowment could very well negate the civil and political rights of liberal democracy that seek to instantiate the dignity that is being unwittingly assaulted. Consequently, any prospect of a posthuman future should be resisted because "we want to protect the full range of our

100

complex, evolved natures against attempts at self-modification. We do not want to disrupt either the unity or the continuity of human nature, and thereby the human rights that are based on it."[19]

Fukuyama's "no" to a posthuman future, and derivatively to regenerative medicine, is, however, subdued. He admits that if biotechnology were only a menace to the bedrock principle of human dignity, then it should be prohibited. Yet he cannot bring himself to make such a recommendation, because he also acknowledges that potentially beneficial therapies can be developed despite the threat. What we are confronting in biotechnology is a "devil's bargain" in which "obvious benefits" are mixed "with subtle harms in one seamless package."[20] Can the benefits be separated from the harms? Fukuyama believes they can by using *the power of the state to regulate*[21] biotechnology. He proposes a series of policies that would assess proposed research in light of the philosophical standard of human dignity summarized above.[22] Since the standard of assessment is also the moral norm to be protected, such research should proceed slowly and cautiously. As a former member of the President's Council on Bioethics, Fukuyama's voting record on embryonic stem cell research and cloning demonstrated that the pace should be very deliberate.

A resounding "no" (Leon Kass)

For Leon Kass, former chairman of the President's Council on Bioethics, the very idea that humans would willingly aspire to become posthuman should prompt a response of repugnance: "No friend of humanity cheers for a posthuman future."[23] A quest for immortality or greatly extended life spans necessarily imperils the mortality and finitude from which meaning and virtue are derived.[24] It is in coming to terms with their finite limits, and the inherent pain and suffering entailed in those limits, that humans embody a nobility of spirit that is supremely expressed in procreation, for the future is properly shaped through progeny rather than extending the lives of the progenitors. "Nothing humanly fine, let alone great, will come out of a society that is willing to sacrifice all other goods to keep the present generation alive and intact. Nothing humanly fine, let alone great, will come from the desire to pursue bodily immortality

101

for ourselves."[25] In short, being and remaining human requires an *absolute* dependence on finitude.[26]

Kass agrees with Fukuyama that the principal issue at stake is preserving human dignity. The former, however, is not merely amplifying the volume of the latter's rhetoric. Kass is far more suspicious and critical of the science and philosophy underlying a posthuman future. Following Hans Jonas, Kass insists that modern science is driven by a relentless desire for mastery and manipulation, exerting maximum control over nature and human nature. Presumably this control will result in greater human freedom, but ironically humans become increasingly enslaved to the tasks required in such mastery, exchanging a capricious nature for fickle engineering.[27] There are few moral brakes to be applied in slowing this momentum, for late moderns have become convinced that there are no normative concepts that define what it means to be human, and therefore no normative ends to be pursued that would preserve their dignity. This moral and spiritual blindness is exemplified in the sorry state of contemporary bioethics that has much to say about freedom and autonomy but nothing about dignity, and whose leading practitioners have created a cottage industry blessing the steady flow of new products tossed into the market by the growing biotechnology industry.[28] For Kass, unlike Hayles and Fukuyama, the great fear of the future "is not tyranny but voluntary dehumanization."[29]

Kass is also less sanguine than Fukuyama that we can sort out the devil's bargain. It may very well prove futile to resist a posthuman future, because of the extent to which we are coming to depend upon and enjoy the blessings of a technologically driven medicine. Humans may therefore lack the moral courage and spiritual fortitude to pursue the hard work of discerning the difference between a hubristic quest for immortality and genuinely compassionate healthcare. Consequently, the advent of regenerative medicine may come to mark a both fateful and fatal step toward a posthuman destination that should be avoided.

But What Question Did These Answers Answer?

The preceding section summarized four replies to the question of whether or not humans should aspire to become posthuman. A spectrum was apparently disclosed, ranging from enthusiastic endorsement to equally robust opposition. Presumably these replies could be used as heuristic markers to plot a range of perspectives that might shed light on various moral responses to current and anticipated developments in regenerative medicine. For example, a correlation might be drawn between the emphasis placed on dignity and any corresponding claims regarding the normative status of the human embryo, which in turn informs various levels of opposition or support for embryonic stem cell research. In this respect, the extent to which an imagined future promotes or denigrates a notion of dignity is expressed in various policy positions, and the fears or concerns reflected in those positions could be dealt with more directly within ensuing debates over proposed public policies.

It would be a mistake, however, to undertake such an endeavor, for it is not clear what question the preceding replies really answered. Although each used the term *posthuman*, they are not necessarily referring to the same thing. It could not be otherwise, for how can one describe what this imagined being, who has capabilities beyond anything currently available, would be like? Consequently, the transhumanists are perplexed about how to describe a virtually immortal being, while Hayles is at a loss to speculate on what the constructed posthuman body might be like; it remains a mystery what exactly Fukuyama wants to avoid through regulation, and what Kass wishes to prevent through prohibition.

Why do these interpretations span the gamut from utopian dream to apocalyptic nightmare? It is in addressing this question that the value of such speculation about the future is disclosed, for the expressed hopes and fears reveal what is preoccupying those who are speculating. In the remainder of this chapter I enucleate this preoccupation by examining how each answer comes to terms with the more immediate relationship between necessity and goodness. I have selected this perennial topic because what is purportedly at stake in becoming posthuman is the extent to which human biology generally, and the human body in particular, is an evil to be overcome or a good to be preserved, and how the resulting efforts to either overcome or consent to the perceived constraints of natural necessity should be assessed. In short, the question of finitude is no more pressing than when pondering the merits and limits of embodiment. By revisiting the various answers within this framework, we can perhaps gain some moral insight on regenerative medicine that might otherwise be missed.

For the purpose of this inquiry, I define "necessity" as the use, acquisition, or consumption of things that are needed to sustain the life of an organism. In regard to humans, these things include air, water, food, exercise, rest, shelter, and the like; and to perpetuate the species, reproduction should be added to the list. None of these things is inherently good or evil, and each of these things is assigned a relative value by those using, acquiring, or consuming them. We do not normally ponder breathing as a moral dilemma, and I may value eating over resting, while you prefer to exercise.

Necessity, however, poses two problems, at least for creatures such as humans, who have the ability to contemplate their fate. First, necessary things sustain the lives of creatures, but these creatures cannot be sustained indefinitely, and necessarily so. Humans are born, grow old, and die. Moreover, it appears that this fatal pattern for individual human beings is necessary to promote the survival of the species. Natural selection has pieced together a human organism that is efficient at breeding but not much else. Consequently, humans need to produce and raise their offspring, and then get out the way to allow the next wave of breeding to run its fateful and fatal course. Once individuals have passed their reproductive potential, evolution has no interest in how much longer they survive.

Second, there is the problem of how necessary things are used, acquired, or consumed. Necessary things are scarce rather then plentiful, and therefore tend to be used, acquired, or consumed in a competitive manner. This competition is both inter- and intraspecies. *Homo sapiens*, for instance, apparently acquired the prerequisite skills to eliminate their Neanderthal competitors, and among humans some individuals are better equipped than others in competing for scarce resources, resulting in a stronger species over time by culling weaker genes from the gene pool.

The preceding summary of these two problems posed by natural necessity is admittedly a sketchy generalization, but it nevertheless serves to demonstrate why the necessary and the good are not synonymous or even complementary concepts. Survival necessarily entails the pain, suffering, and morbidity associated with mortality.

Although the death of an individual benefits one's offspring directly, and the species more generally, it is nonetheless perverse to designate this fate as being good. Even Christians who ardently long for the new life in Christ over the old life of sin nonetheless correctly identify death as the final enemy. Moreover, competitive violence and carnage have been amplified to nearly unspeakable levels with the growth of late modern civil communities. Although poverty or war may prove to benefit some at the expense of others, it would again be perverse to claim that they are good. In short, one cannot simply assert that because something is necessary it is therefore good, much less that something is good because it is necessary.

Many philosophers and theologians have tried to relieve this stark tension between the necessary and the good. The Hegelian and Marxist solution, for example, is that history settles the issue. Hegelians try to transform necessity into goodness; the good is self-realized through freedom that overcomes the necessary. This freedom is achieved through progressive historical acts that culminate in the absolute state, reflecting a human mastery of nature and human nature. Consequently, there are no constraints on human acts that strive to realize this perfected state of freedom. Marxists take a similar path, but the goal is to achieve a classless society as the epitome of perfect freedom. The objective at stake is a social rather than political one. In either case, the pain and suffering inflicted in achieving the goal is justified because it is necessary for obtaining the greater good of the absolute state or classless society.

The weakness of this approach is that it exchanges natural necessity with historical necessity, thereby amplifying the scope of suffering and misery entailed in perfecting human freedom. The move virtually justifies force as a redemptive tool in which goodness and necessity become the fabric of attenuated notions of progress and providence. This move, however, results in a cavalier attitude toward evil, for acts of cruelty and violence are justified by historical necessity, but it is a denuded justice that is invoked, for the good of the powerful is achieved at the expense of the weak. As George Grant has written: "The screams of the tortured child can be justified by the achievements of history. How pleasant for the achievers, but how meaningless for the child."[30] The hope that human action can achieve the good by replacing natural necessity with historical

105

necessity is delusional. Grant goes on to assert that any invocation of historical progress "is blasphemy if it rests on any easy identification of necessity and good."[31]

In opposition to this blasphemy, Grant proposes an alternative Platonic-Christian understanding of the relation between goodness and necessity. Following Simone Weil, Grant contends that the Creator withdraws from creation to give its creatures genuine freedom as an act of absolute love. The creation and its creatures become something truly other than God, and therefore a proper object of God's love. This withdrawal, however, subjects the creatures to the constraints of necessity, which negates their freedom. Necessity distributes misery, violence, and disease "in accordance with its own proper mechanism."[32] An infinite chasm separates the necessary from the good, and it cannot be bridged by any human action. Humans cannot erase or redeem their tragic history on their own terms. In Weil's beguiling words, "God's absence is the most marvelous testimony of perfect love, and that's why pure necessity, the necessity which is manifestly so different from good, is so beautiful."[33] How do we come to terms with a necessity whose beauty is devoid of goodness? According to Grant, we must learn to love our fate and consent to the limits it imposes. This love does not result in sullen resignation but opens us to the same love that makes necessity beautiful. Although the necessary and the good can never be joined, the chasm separating them has been bridged by the suffering of Christ as the incarnate mediator.[34] We consent to necessity in obedience to God, and the resulting love of fate enables a love of neighbor expressed in the recognition of a fundamental equality and indifferent compassion. This is the best that can be achieved on this beautiful side of the chasm, for the good can embrace us only on the other, eternal side. In the meantime, this eschatological hope is best expressed, following Martin Luther, in affirming a theology of the cross that consents to necessity instead of a theology of glory that tries vainly to transform it into goodness.[35]

Kass seemingly favors Grant's Platonic-Christian account over the Hegelian–Marxist option—up to a point, and it is a significant point of departure. If regenerative medicine is driven by a quest for extending longevity or virtual immortality, then it represents little more than another vain attempt to transform necessity into goodness.

Indeed, exchanging natural necessity with technological necessity can have no good effect, because it corrupts medicine as an art that should help individuals to struggle with rather than eliminate finite limits. If medicine dedicates itself to waging a war against death, then it must also come to hate the very human body it allegedly serves because its finitude prevents any final victory. Medicine, then, should properly limit its practices to assisting patients to come to terms with lineage, parenthood, and embodiment, as finite endeavors entailing suffering and eventual death.[36] In this respect, medicine is properly an intergenerational institution preserving human dignity by assisting a morally integral process of biological and social reproduction.[37] Any attempt to become posthuman is therefore a hubristic effort to remove the necessary limits that provide the natural foundations of human dignity.

Although we may say, in Grant's and Weil's terms, that Kass acknowledges the beauty of necessity, his subsequent consent is only partial. Necessity's beauty does not confer to nature any absolute sovereignty over the structure of human life. Kass readily admits there are no pretechnological good old days to recover, and there is nothing wrong with medicine helping people live long lives surrounded by loving children and grandchildren. The biblical three-score-and-ten is a flexible rule of thumb, rather than a rigid limit, gently reminding humans of their mortality, and hence the pressing need for natality. This flexibility, however, presents a dilemma: at what point does medicine cross the line, becoming a hubristic attempt to transform necessity into goodness, and thereby forsaking the art of helping patients come to terms with their finitude and mortality? Kass is hard pressed to draw this line at any particular location, for he also argues that there is nothing wrong in developing more effective medical treatments. Yet if the research underlying regenerative medicine is prohibited, then is not the resulting suffering that could have been prevented justified by the necessity of willful restraint? Seemingly the pain and suffering of the few are justified to preserve the dignity of the many. In addition, his objection to regenerative medicine is not to its therapeutic and preventive goals per se, but to the production and cloning of embryos to harvest their stem cells. If the same results could be achieved through extracting adult stem cells, then he would be hard-pressed to object, because greater longevity would be a secondary effect of better therapeutic and preventive measures. So long as the willful destruction of embryos is avoided, cannot humans enjoy longer and healthier lives with their dignity intact?

Moreover, the object of Kass's hope for the future is offspring, in terms of perpetuating the species as well as protecting human dignity. This means, however, that the chasm separating necessity and goodness can neither be reconciled nor bridged. Procreation and children are instead asserted as goods in their own right, albeit in a diminished form, because such a strategy can only fail in embracing an eternal good that lies beyond a chasm that has never been and can never be traversed. Through lineage humans may achieve a sense of immortality but will never encounter eternity. Although any grand scheme of transforming the necessary into the good should be rejected, lesser, temporary niches of goodness can be carved out through the bonds of lineage, kinship, and descent. This is perhaps the best Kass can offer, because, as Gerald McKenny has observed, he lacks a clear understanding of medicine's moral authority and therefore can offer only a narrow and prudent vision of the good it purports to be pursuing.[38]

Of the authors surveyed, it is, surprisingly, Hayles who shares the greatest affinity with Kass. This claim is admittedly counterintuitive, for it would appear that her ambiguous "yes" and his resounding "no" to the prospect of becoming posthuman would place them in opposing camps. Yet when the question is posed in terms of necessity and goodness, Hayles shares with Kass an unflinching opposition to any program that attempts to negate human embodiment and finitude. Although in celebrating embodied finitude Hayles is unwilling to invoke or protect normative values such as dignity, she is nonetheless prepared to resist any effort that threatens the survival of embodied persons. Presumably, at some point, then, she is also prepared to draw a line specifying the extent to which the technological transformation of humans may proceed but must not pass, even though she is unwilling to specify in advance where that line might be drawn. Where Hayles differs with Kass is that the great enemy to be resisted is neither Hegel nor Marx and their respective myths of the absolute state and classless society, but a more pernicious liberal humanism and its myth of autonomy as exemplified by the transhumanists. Thus, the small niches of goodness that are to be carved out within a realm of necessity involve the construction of posthumans that have preserved the value of finite embodiment, rather than preserving a so-called dignity derived from lineage and kinship. Consequently, for Hayles the pressing task at hand is not biological and social reproduction, but constructing a social and political order that genuinely enables the survival of its inhabitants.

Since the issue for Hayles is not whether a posthuman future will emerge, but rather what kind of posthumans should be constructed to populate the future, she is ambivalent about the prospect of regenerative medicine. Given the constructive task at hand, the development of embryonic stem cell research, cloning, and prosthetic enhancements is neither inherently good nor inherently bad. The concern at stake is one of application: regenerative medicine may produce tools that either assist or impede the construction of finite and embodied posthumans, with the resulting challenge to discern the difference between the two. It is this presumption of instrumental neutrality, however, that imperils Hayles's program. Since she is unwilling to specify in advance any normative values that are derived from embodied finitude, early forays into regenerative medicine may generate an unwanted momentum that cannot be effectively resisted, much less stopped. As Grant argues, technology is not a neutral set of instruments from which we may pick and choose. Rather, it is a way of life that enfolds its users in its own destiny, thereby transforming or disfiguring what the very meaning of goodness comes to mean. To partake of technology generally, and medical technologies in particular, necessarily entails a package deal in which any so-called freedom that picking and choosing purportedly enables is little more than a cruel illusion.[39] Technology shapes its users in its image, and not vice versa. In partaking of regenerative medicine's early fruits to construct her posthuman future, Hayles may be starting down a road whose inevitable destination is the transhumanist vision she wishes to resist.

Transhumanists are dedicated to transforming humans into posthumans because they can discern no aesthetic qualities in the realm of natural necessity. There is nothing beautiful about mortality. This is not a fate to be embraced, but one to be resisted and conquered at all costs. To do otherwise is to succumb to a death wish, to consent to extinction. Correspondingly, transhumanists also have no interest

109

in natality, for the birth of a child serves as a reminder of necessity's death and decay. The task at hand is neither Kass's biological and social reproduction nor Hayles's social and political construction, but a frenetic and continuous transformation and projection of the self as far as possible, or better, endlessly into the future. Since evolution has not equipped humans to successfully complete this chore, they must take its future course into their own hands. Consequently, a relentless war against death can and should be waged, and the advent of regenerative medicine is to be welcomed as the initial salvo against this foe. The current and anticipated fruits of biotechnology and nanotechnology, for instance, should be neither forbidden nor eaten selectively, but consumed voraciously to strengthen individuals for the battles that lie ahead. Those seeking to prohibit or restrict the requisite research and experimentation should be regarded as the true enemies of humanity, for in trying to preserve a so-called dignity or celebrate the values of finitude, they are conspiring with the enemy. In this respect, transhumanists have raised the ante on Hegel and Marx: the genuine good of freedom cannot be attained in either the absolute state or the classless society, but only in the virtually immortal posthuman. It is only when mortality has been vanquished that humans are truly free. Thus, whatever scientific and political means are required to wage an effective war against death are justified by the historical necessity of achieving this perfect freedom.

In appealing to immortality, however, transhumanists tip their hand. Despite their rhetoric, they cannot really claim a humanistic pedigree. No humanist would willfully consent to transforming humanity to the extent that its ceases to be human, for this would destroy both the measure and the goal of the moral enterprise undertaken, namely, to be fully and therefore *only* human. Transhumanists also harbor a death wish of transforming *Homo sapiens* into extinction, in order that the posthuman can emerge. Yet it is far from clear if creatures dedicated to the suicide of their species can think any more rationally about the moral, social, and political implications of regenerative medicine than can those consenting to eventual extinction through natural selection. More tellingly, the immortality they seek will not grant the kind of mastery they desire. Even within Greek mythology the immortals are not eternal, and they therefore remain subject to a fate they cannot control. Rather than bridging the chasm separating necessity and goodness, transhumanists are endeavoring to dig it deeper and wider. Consequently, they have not raised the ante on Hegel and Marx but have swept them aside in favor of Nietzsche. His hope of the *Übermensch* is now possible with the advent of sophisticated technologies. Their adulation, however, is limited, for unlike in Nietzsche, the prerequisite for the emergence of this new being is not a love of fate, but rather the outcome of engineering designed to negate fate. The transhumanists, therefore, have bet everything on technological development. But how will these high-tech nihilists respond if their initial steps through regenerative medicine propel them toward a destination that can only disappoint? Specifically, what happens if death proves to be an unconquerable enemy, and they are left with a necessity that remains a fate they cannot love? In Grant's words, they "will be resolute in their will to mastery, but they cannot know what that mastery is for."[40] Given the technological power that will presumably be at their disposal, one shudders to think what might occur if these nihilists conclude that it is better to will nothing when there is nothing good to will.

It is such an apocalyptic specter that Fukuyama wants to avoid by regulating the research underlying regenerative medicine. His rationale for justifying such regulation is straightforward: natural selection has produced a species called human that is capable of developing and sustaining liberal democratic societies. This is no small blessing, since such societies go a long way in softening the sharp edges of natural necessity. In this respect, some aspects of beauty within the necessary can be perceived, yet these perceptions should prompt us neither to love nor to overcome fate. Fukuyama makes no attempt to bridge the chasm separating necessity and goodness, but we catch glimpses of universal goods through natural law, which in turn should order our moral, social, and political lives. Our understanding and institutional ordering of these goods have emerged from our natural evolution as a species, so we should be wary of unwittingly unraveling an evolutionary process that to date has served humankind well and should not be casually disregarded. The therapies and enhancements envisioned by proponents of regenerative medicine will alter the human species over time. Consequently, such interventions should be deployed only in a highly judicious manner, so that the natural foundations of liberal democracy are not inadvertently undermined. Such caution may consign some individuals to pain and suffering, but their fate is justified by the necessity of preserving the greater good of civil society. In short, necessity dictates prudence to preserve the temporal goods that have already been obtained.

At first glance it appears that Fukuyama has slammed the door shut on any posthuman future. Yet in opting for regulating instead of prohibiting research, he has left the door open a crack, and in examining that small space we discover an unexpected affinity with the transhumanists. Fukuyama favors regulation over prohibition because he recognizes that some aspects of regenerative medicine may prove to be genuinely beneficial. In facing the devil's bargain he leaves open the possibility that we might be able to outfox this crafty adversary; hence, the slow and cautious approach. If the devil can be outfoxed, however, then what differentiates Fukuyama from the transhumanists are not any normative claims about human nature, but the pace of transforming humans into posthumans. This is where his confidence in natural selection betrays his normative rhetoric. The goods that natural law purportedly discloses are not given but emerge from the evolutionary process itself. Thus, these goods are self-referential rather than revelatory of a transcendent or eternal source. The evolution of *Homo sapiens* is also open-ended. One cannot point to a particular point of evolutionary development and proclaim "this far but no further," for change or mutation is precisely what enables a species to flourish and avoid extinction. Yet if humans evolve over time, then so too do the emergent goods disclosed in natural law, because they are themselves derived from the underlying evolutionary process. Consequently, a posthuman future cannot be foreclosed in advance on Fukuyama's own evolutionary terms. As judicious interventions are introduced through carefully regulated therapies and enhancements, they will still have a cumulative effect over time, thereby effectively transforming humans. If these interventions should prove to offer no substantive threat to the so-called natural foundations of liberal democracy, then he would be hard-pressed to argue for the superiority of natural selection over willfully directed evolution. The goods revealed by his emergent natural law may in fact evolve to a point where they dictate the necessity of humans exerting greater control over their evolutionary fate. Fukuyama must be open to this prospect, for, unlike Kass, such things as procreation, lineage, and embodiment are not the foundations of human dignity, but the *currently* necessary means of perpetuating liberal democratic societies that in turn bestow dignity to their citizens. If initial forays into the technological transformation of humans should prove unthreatening to the social and political sources of this dignity, then Fukuyama cannot entirely foreclose the possibility and desirability of a posthuman future, especially if it is populated by more proficient democrats. In short, the necessity of evolution dictates that *Homo sapiens* will become something other than human, and presumably this change can occur through unhurried natural selection or hasty technological transformation. Fukuyama prefers the former but is also hedging that preference by not foreclosing the latter.

Postscript

The purpose of this chapter is to examine how broader philosophical considerations might inform the more discrete moral debates associated with the advent of regenerative medicine. Moral deliberation on such issues as embryonic stem cell research, cloning, and prosthetics is conducted within a larger constellation of basic convictions and beliefs. What this inquiry has disclosed, however, is that these formative considerations do not produce a monolithic range of predictable attitudes regarding regenerative medicine but, to the contrary, reveal varying fault lines depending on what type of question is being asked. The affinities in answering the question of whether or not humans should aspire to become posthuman, for example, do not hold when applied to the question of how necessity and goodness are related. Consequently, philosophical and theological inquiries into questions of human origin and destiny need to be conducted in tandem with more discrete inquiries to identify the logical trajectories of various arguments. Otherwise, we run the risk of using regenerative medicine in an ad hoc manner that may produce an inhospitable future for either its eventual human or posthuman inhabitants.

Most importantly, this exercise discloses the limits of philosophical discourse if Christians are, *as Christians*, to make substantive

113

contributions to bioethics. This is particularly the case in respect to regenerative medicine, and more broadly the prospect of posthuman transformation. To address these concerns properly, normative claims must be made regarding human beings as finite, mortal, and embodied creatures, and what their hope and destiny as such thereby entail. Consequently, Christian discourse on bioethics must be philosophically astute, but it is ultimately a theological mode of inquiry and exposition that is grounded in scripture, doctrine, and worship. The following chapters explore what explicating an overtly Christian bioethics might entail.

6

What Is Christian about Christian Bioethics?

The short answer to this question is, of course, Jesus Christ. If, however, this answer is to be informative rather than glib, something more needs to be said. A comprehensive explication is beyond the scope of this chapter, so for the sake of clarity my inquiry is confined to some basic claims that are derived from the incarnation. This doctrine provides a promising starting point, for what Christians believe about the Word made flesh presumably shapes their normative convictions regarding the purpose and practice of medicine. Moreover, it is a timely doctrine to revisit, given medicine's growing predilection for turning its attention away from the care of patients in favor of transforming them into beings capable of transcending their embodied, and therefore finite, limitations. It is on setting this context that we first turn our attention.

Late Modern Medicine

As was noted in the preceding chapter, as late moderns we are purportedly entering a golden age of healthcare. Under the broad rubric of "regenerative medicine," biotechnology, nanotechnology, and various information technologies are being combined to develop highly efficacious therapies. Recent discoveries in human genetics are enabling more effective treatments of a growing spectrum of diseases and disabilities. Nanotechnology is already being utilized in treating heart disease, and shows great promise in overcoming the debilitating constraints of a wide range of compromised organs and biological processes. Prosthetics controlled by the mind have restored the mobility and dexterity of various recipients and have partially reversed the ill effects of brain damage. It is reasonable to assume that the pace of future technological development and sophistication will quicken.

These therapeutic advances are accompanied by a number of moral controversies. Embryonic stem cell research and therapeutic cloning underlying anticipated breakthroughs in biomedicine have generated the most hotly contested disputes. The disputants and their chief arguments are well known and need not be rehearsed for the purpose of this chapter.[1] A more subtle, yet arguably prescient, issue is that various therapies can also be used to enhance physical and cognitive performance.[2] Drugs designed to treat sleeping or behavioral disorders, for instance, can also be used to intensify alertness. Synthetic devices replacing diseased or damaged organs can be employed to augment the performance of healthy ones. The same technology underlying the creation of artificial limbs and restoring damaged mental capacities can be deployed to increase the strength and dexterity of healthy limbs and to enhance the capabilities of undamaged brains.

Although the advent of regenerative medicine has not erased the line separating therapy and enhancement, it has certainly blurred it. This blurring is admittedly not a novel development, and regenerative medicine may be characterized as intensifying the transition in modern healthcare from care to cure.[3] Throughout much of history, medicine provided little more than care by ameliorating, as best it could, the pain and suffering of the dying and desperately ill. Beginning roughly in the early twentieth century, medicine became more proficient at curing or preventing a wide range of debilitating and life-threatening diseases. The most vivid indication of this change in emphasis, at least in industrialized nations, has been a dramatic increase in longevity. This indicator also discloses the extent to which the line separating therapy and enhancement has already faded, for living longer and healthier lives can be described as an enhancement in comparison with the expectations and experience of previous generations.

Presumably, few would quarrel with the outcomes of this transition. Yet there is a troubling consequence of emphasizing cure and prevention over care that should give some pause. Medicine is arguably a public demonstration of how civil communities maintain their association with the ill and infirm. Medicine is the social bridge over which the healthy keep company with the dying and debilitated.[4] Providing such care, however, also indicates medicine's embarrassing failure either to prevent or to cure. This embarrassment is removed by increasingly diminishing the necessity for such care as witnessed by medicine's central role in identifying and destroying "defective" embryos and fetuses, and its declining reticence to perform euthanasia and assist suicide. The resulting healthcare system would, ideally, not need to offer care, other than for brief periods of recuperation and rehabilitation. The bridge linking the healthy and the ill should be a narrow and temporary one.

The narrowing of this bridge casts the principal benefit of regenerative medicine in a problematic light. As new therapies and enhancements are developed, longevity will continue to increase, perhaps dramatically. In turn, more medical resources will be devoted to treating and preventing diseases and infirmities associated with aging. Many of the therapies and enhancements currently being developed to prevent deteriorating physical strength and mental functions, as noted above, are well suited to achieve these goals. One result, however, is that medicine is not so much interested in assisting intergenerational transitions through biological and social reproduction as it is in preserving the hegemony of a current generation over a new one for as long as possible. As the term *regenerative* connotes, the primary objective shifts toward self-renewal rather than toward creating future possibilities. This shift is seen in the concurrent development of so-called reproductive medicine in which the principal goals are either to prevent or to assist the births of unwanted and wanted babies, respectively, and to control the qualitative outcomes satisfying the personal interests of those commissioning reproductive projects.[5] In this respect, the resulting product is a projection of the commissioner(s) will to create or otherwise obtain a child. It is an attempt to control or determine the future rather than bequeathing a possibility, for the latter requires that the present pass away to allow the possible to be realized; mortality and natality must be integrally related if they are to be genuinely productive.[6]

In asserting this hegemony of the present over the future, increased longevity mutates from a benefit to an encompassing goal. Consequently, aging itself is coming to be regarded as if it were a disease to be treated. But, as was noted in the previous chapter, what would it mean to cure aging? This is an admittedly awkward question, but it is surely the right one to ask, since medicine has already, at least conceptually, moved away from care as its raison d'être. In asking this question, however, we must be clear about what is at stake. The issue is not living longer per se. There is little evidence we may draw upon to suggest that extending the human life span significantly—and we need not indulge the transhumanist dream of virtual immortality to pursue this imaginative inquiry but may allow the reader to define what constitutes a significant increase—would necessarily result in a dramatic redefinition of the human condition. Social, political, and economic institutions have already demonstrated an ability to adapt themselves to the needs of an aging population. This is why objections to extending longevity by appealing to the unrelenting boredom and subjective stagnation that living substantially longer lives would entail are not convincing.[7] Late moderns have proven to be adept at keeping these evils at bay through voracious production and insatiable consumption, a feat achieved in a populace that already enjoys, in comparison to previous generations, dramatically increased longevity. In this respect, what regenerative medicine offers is a benefit of degree instead of kind.

Rather, the issue at hand is that if aging is to be cured, then the patient must be radically transformed. If the success of regenerative medicine is measured by its ability to both extend longevity and preserve and enhance physical and mental performance, then it will eventually reach the limits of human biology. And if a cure for aging has no outside limit, short of immortality, then continuing success will require medicine to go beyond these biological limits. Artificial exoskeletons, for instance, may someday offer greater strength and agility than that afforded by muscle enhancement drugs; nanotechnology may enable the construction of more efficient and durable organs; direct neuro-links to information networks may prove more productive and desirable than chemical stimulants. This is why therapeutic and enhancement prosthetics are already part of regenerative medicine's currently modest cornucopia. As various therapies and enhancements grow increasingly efficacious, the indirect benefit of increased longevity will emerge as a principal expectation and objective of healthcare.

From Flesh to Data

In waging a war against finitude, which aging literally embodies, medicine is, perhaps unwittingly, enfolded into posthuman discourse. Posthuman discourse is based on the underlying science of cybernetics.[8] Cybernetics was initially confined to the study of complex feedback loops within both organisms and mechanisms and their larger environments. More expansively, cybernetics reduces organisms and mechanisms to underlying information that, in theory, can be digitized and therefore reconfigured. Consequently, any so-called definitive borders or boundaries can, in principle, be erased and redrawn at will if sufficient technological capability is available. If medicine is to wage an effective war against aging, then it must develop therapies and enhancements that redraw the boundaries separating the organic from the mechanistic, and the natural from the artificial. The patient is thereby simultaneously the beneficiary and the artifact of medical interventions. The success of regenerative medicine in particular is predicated on its ability to transform humans into posthuman cyborgs.

Once medicine is shaped by posthuman discourse, it also embraces the historicist task of constructing, rather than conforming to, reality.[9] In undertaking this task there is no reason to assume that the creators of reality cannot recreate themselves in the process as well. Presumably, the cost of this transformation is justified by extended longevity and enhanced physical and mental capabilities. In this respect, regenerative medicine represents improved engineering of the inefficient prosthetics bequeathed to humans by biological evolution.

119

It may appear that posthuman discourse represents a radical departure from traditional modes of thought. Yet it is arguable that in many respects it denotes a logical extension of the late modern attempt to master nature and human nature. This continuity can be seen by visiting briefly the interrelated philosophical and theological topics of the relationships among necessity, goodness, temporality, and eternity.

Reiterating and expanding upon the previous chapter's discussion, *necessity* is a shorthand term referring to those things and conditions required to sustain human life and enable it to flourish over time. Natural necessity includes such biological needs as air, sustenance, shelter, and procreation, whereas historical necessity denotes cultural, social, and political institutions promoting an easier and more efficient satisfaction of these needs that endure across generations. Any form of human existence beyond mere survival is therefore predicated on varying abilities to master natural environments and processes. Or, in more contemporary parlance, human life marks a nexus of biological and cultural evolution.

Although these necessary things and conditions sustain human life over time, they are also the source of pain and suffering. At the natural level, for instance, there is seemingly a scarcity of resources necessitating a relentless and often brutal competition, both between and within particular species. *Homo sapiens* were apparently more proficient hunters, and perhaps better killers, than their Neanderthal competitors. Among humans, some individuals are more adept at surviving, often at the expense of their compatriots. In both cases survival and flourishing are predicated upon suffering, pain, and death. The extinction of an inferior species promotes the flourishing of a superior one, and the demise of weak individuals benefits the interests of the strong.

A similar pattern seems to be repeated in the realm of historical necessity. Economic, social, and political structures can produce only a limited number of goods and services to be consumed, again necessitating relentless and often brutal competition. Traditional cultures are usually overwhelmed when they encounter more technologically advanced ones. The production and consumption of various goods and services apparently enrich some individuals while impoverishing others.

Moreover, necessity, in both its natural and historical forms, is accompanied by futility. To partake of the necessary things and conditions that promote survival and flourishing is a temporal activity that has no permanence or lasting quality. The strongest individuals grow old and die; once-dominant species become extinct; cultures rise and fall. At best, humans create and utilize temporal goods, but they can never embrace the eternal Good. Although these temporal goods may reflect, to varying degrees, the Good, it can never be fully embodied within the realm of temporal necessity. Hence, Simone Weil's beguiling observation that necessity is beautiful but can never be good, for goodness resides on the eternal bank of an immense gulf separating it from the necessary side in which human life is enmeshed.[10]

Traditional responses to this predicament most often entailed some sort of consent to necessary finite and temporal limits. The Platonic solution, for example, is to learn to love the fate dictated by these constraints. In other words, life is preparation for death. A rare philosopher might have sufficient vision to catch a glimpse of the Good on the eternal side of the chasm, but seeing is not crossing. It is only in death that the soul is freed to be embraced by the eternal Good. In the meantime, one must rest content with a love of fate fashioned in the image of a beautiful necessity and futile finitude.

An alternative, though complementary, Augustinian solution is to contend that the chasm separating temporal necessity and eternal goodness has been bridged. The initiative for this bridging is undertaken exclusively from the eternal side as revealed in the suffering and death of Jesus Christ as the incarnate reconciler. Consequently, acts of temporal necessity are not futile because they are performed by beings who already participate in the eternal life of their Creator and Redeemer. The bridge between necessity and goodness is thereby not designed to accommodate two-way traffic, but is a means for those sharing the suffering and death of the reconciler to be resurrected into God's eternity. The task, then, is not to approximate the Good in a love of fate, but to love God who in turn redeems acts of temporal necessity from their futility.

In contrast, the late modern solution is to simply negate the good and the eternal. There are no given or definitive limits to constrain the scope of temporal and finite aspirations. Humans do not encounter

121

an absolute chasm, but an ever-expanding horizon of imaginative potential. What, it might be asked, prevents this horizon from becoming a nihilistic abyss? The modern solution was to concoct a notion of progress to guide the exploration and settlement of this new, unlimited landscape. Undertaking this historicist project, however, required a strategy of mastering nature and human nature,[11] for in the absence of any eternal Good, humans can at least establish temporal goods that endure over relatively extensive periods of time. In this respect, natural necessity is displaced by historical necessity. This displacement eased an anxious futility, for in constructing a progressive history humans participate in a fabricated reality transcending their finitude and temporality. In the absence of eternity, the artifact of history offers a kind of immortality to fill the void. Hegel's absolute state and Marx's classless society, respectively, represent the high-water marks of modern attempts to construct a fate that humans could more easily learn to love, because such a fate was the fruit of their own labor.

Late moderns (aka postmoderns) agree that all historical horizons are imaginative projections, but they dismiss progress as a ghost of the fictitious eternal Good. We enter this landscape with no guide or even compass. Consequently, there is no progressive metanarrative to be written, only an endless array of emerging autobiographical vignettes. The late modern social reality is a realm of constantly shifting borders and boundaries to accommodate a populous of self-authoring beings. There is, then, no transcendent reality, either given or constructed, that can provide a sense of immortality. Rather, the only effective strategy for easing the futility of finite and temporal existence is to construct social realities and their inhabitants in ways that promote survival and self-defined flourishing for as long as possible. Technology thereby becomes the principal instrument for implementing this survival ethic of social and self-construction. In this respect, natural and historical necessity are subsumed into an imperative to be tirelessly self-creative,[12] for the ideal goal is to create a condition in which birth and death are matters of choice and not necessity.

What does this all have to do with bioethics? Within the modern project of producing a progressive and immortal history, medicine took the lead in fulfilling the prerequisite mastering of nature and human nature. The finite and temporal good of healthcare, especially its focus on ordering natality and mortality, was the chief means of subsuming natural necessity into its historical counterpart, albeit to a limited extent given technological constraints. Medicine, therefore, was a premier institution and practice for ordering both biological and social reproduction.

With the so-called postmodern shift, medicine became a means of constructing and asserting a wide range of idiosyncratic narratives as opposed to an overarching progressive metanarrative. Rather than an institution and a practice ordering biological and social reproduction, healthcare is a dispenser of medical commodities that assist individuals and communities to simultaneously author and enact their respective stories. In consuming these commodities, "patients" exert greater control in achieving the goals of making birth and death matters of choice rather than necessity, as witnessed by greater and easier recourse to reproductive technologies enabling improved quality control, elective reconstructive surgeries, and euthanasia and assisted suicide. In this respect, anticipated advances in regenerative medicine complement this postmodern shift by enhancing the longevity and productive quality of the author/actor.

Through its instantiation in this shift, medicine becomes embedded in posthuman discourse. If there are no given limits to the extent that the lives of individuals can be extended and enhanced, then patients, as noted above, will not only benefit but also be transformed in consuming their selected medical commodities. Moreover, this transformation is justified by the posthuman imperative to assist individual survival and flourishing for as long as possible. If healthcare is a principal means of subsuming natural and historical necessity into the transformative imperative, then it must strive to achieve the ideal goal in which no unwanted child or child with unwanted characteristics is born, and death is a personal response to a life that its author has judged to be no longer worth enacting.

By failing to come to terms with this transformative imperative underlying posthuman discourse, objections appealing to either biological essentialism or innate human dignity are bound to fail.[13] It is difficult to make a convincing case that there is a normative biological human condition that should not be violated once the efficacy of medicine is admitted. The advent of late modern therapies

123

and enhancements has made the lives of many humans arguably more, rather than less, humane. Any line restricting further medical intervention is drawn arbitrarily. Moreover, appealing to an innate dignity that is violated by transforming humans into posthumans is also appealing to the moving and uncertain target of evolution. It is again difficult to make a convincing case that relying on natural selection, as opposed to technological transformation, is somehow a more reliable bastion protecting human dignity. Indeed, the central premise of posthuman discourse is that technological self-transformation is a prerequisite for maximizing latent human potential, especially in respect to freedom. The good to be enjoyed is the product of a transformative project rather than a metaphysical given.

If Christians are to challenge the posthuman imperative of self-transformation, they must resist the temptation of appealing to the dead-end arguments of biological essentialism or inherent dignity. Rather, they must offer an alternative form of discourse that is cognizant of the postmodern shift but rejects its proclivity toward posthuman rhetoric. One promising route for developing this alternative form of discourse is to critically reappropriate the gulf separating the necessary from the good, and framing the temporal and finite within the eternal. Such discourse is neither modern nor postmodern, because the principal images invoked are not organic, mechanistic, or cybernetic, but christological. Such moral discourse, then, is also theological, for it challenges the posthuman imperative as a false salvific promise; namely, the task at hand is not to extract and organize data from malleable flesh, but to be conformed to the Word made flesh. Christians can readily agree with posthumans that humans will be transformed, but the operative goal is not self-transformation but to become transformed in and by Christ. The remainder of this chapter explores briefly some selected implications that such christological discourse might offer for shaping a bioethics that claims to be Christian.

Word Made Flesh

The present task in developing this christological discourse is *not* simply to incorporate the good example of Jesus's life, teaching, and

124

ministry as formative features of contemporary bioethics. Although I have argued elsewhere that the tension between Jesus's roles as suffering servant and healer may be profitably employed in deliberating on a number of bioethical issues,[14] such recourse is insufficient in itself to challenge the central salvific claim underlying posthuman discourse, namely, that whatever "good" humans may enjoy is directly proportional to the maximization of latent potential that is realized by effectively implementing the transformative imperative. Or, reduced to a slogan: salvation through self-transformation. Rather, the emphasis of this exploration concentrates on the death, resurrection, and exaltation of Jesus Christ as the three-part act culminating the incarnation. Or, posed as a question: how might Good Friday, Easter Sunday, and Ascension Day shape the basic pattern of a *Christian* bioethics? In offering a short provisional answer to this question, I draw heavily on the work of Oliver O'Donovan.[15]

According to O'Donovan, the resurrection of Jesus Christ from the dead is the centerpiece of Christian moral deliberation and discourse. There are two reasons why this is the case. First, in raising Jesus from the dead, God vindicated Jesus's life. Moreover, since God is incarnate in this life, the vindication extends to all of creation. Since humans were not "allowed to uncreate what God created,"[16] there is a created moral order that may be discerned because it has been vindicated by its Creator. Consequently, the resurrection cannot be invoked as a moral principle in isolation from the crucifixion, for otherwise, Easter Sunday is simply the validation of one man, and not the vindication of a creation that the incarnate one came to save.

Second, in raising Jesus from the dead, God disclosed creation's destiny. A vindicated creation does not imply that attention is fixated solely on origin and subsequent history. There is a proleptic trajectory revealed in the resurrection of the incarnate one, disclosing creation's destiny in the exalted Christ and his parousia. Consequently, the resulting ethic is teleological rather than restorationist, for God's vindicated creation is not headed toward a return to Eden, but toward a New Jerusalem. Creation and its creatures will be transformed over time, and human acts will contribute toward this transformation. But it is a transformation shaped by creation's *telos* in Christ, and not by attempts to overcome the limits of natural and historical

125

necessities. The Creator who vindicates a temporal creation will also redeem it in the fullness of time. Again, the resurrection cannot be invoked in isolation from the ascension; otherwise, Easter Sunday is merely an anomaly and not *the* sign of a created order that has been redeemed by the incarnate one.

Two salient strands of O'Donovan's theological framework lend themselves in particular to this inquiry. First, his "natural ethic"[17] overcomes the voluntarist and historicist presumptions of posthuman discourse. Since a divine order encompasses all of creation, its underlying order provides an objective reference point for moral deliberation. Contrary to posthuman discourse, moral judgments are not acts one is free to either perform or refrain from performing. Rather, one may choose to either conform to or rebel against an objective moral order. "The way the universe *is,* determines how man *ought* to behave himself in it."[18] Consequently, moral truth is not the exclusive possession of Christians, suggesting that there are certain virtues that should be practiced by all humans within a created order. Human nature, malleable or otherwise, has no meaning if there is no larger nature within which it is embedded, and from which normative principles can be derived. In this respect, O'Donovan shares an affinity with natural law, but he does not believe that normative principles can be discerned and applied in the absence of revelation. It is in and through Christ that nature, which Christians properly name "creation," discloses its vindicated order that can then be discerned.

This revelatory dimension leads to O'Donovan's second strand of freedom.[19] With Christ's resurrection "we look not only back to the created order" but also "forwards to our eschatological participation in that order."[20] In the absence of this theological vision, humans are enslaved to a false perception of nature in which any natural moral order can only be encountered as threat. The finite and temporal limits of one's condition as a creature are thereby inimical to one's survival and flourishing. Hence the posthuman imperative to overcome these threatening limits through a process of self-transformation. This process is based on the false presumption that it expands the range of freedom by extending finite and temporal limits. The project is thereby enslaving, for it leads to the "incapacity to obey,"[21] and as incapacitated creatures, humans disfigure their proper dominion of creation into a domination of nature in encountering the threats of finitude and temporality. Anticipating our eschatological participation in creation's destiny, however, these threats are exposed as given limits that define and order our lives; we are free to love our fate, because it has already been taken up into the eternal life of our Creator and Redeemer. In this respect, true freedom is a gift of the Spirit that frees us to be obedient to the definitive limits that delineate our lives as finite and mortal creatures.

These strands of a natural ethic and freedom enable a more penetrating critique of the false salvific claim underlying posthuman rhetoric by offering a counter christological form of discourse. One basic contour of this discourse can be sketched out by revisiting the previous discussion on necessity, goodness, temporality, and eternity with these two strands in mind.

As argued above, appeals to biological essentialism and innate human dignity are ineffectual objections to the self-transformation imperative driving posthuman discourse, because in the former instance no substantive claims can be made once the efficacy of medical intervention per se is admitted, and in the latter case the central claim loses any substantive content, given evolutionary change. The net result is that finitude no longer imposes any normative and definitive limits but is simply a barrier to be overcome and mastered. The late modern strategy is to reject the categories of the good and the eternal that allowed the problems of necessity and temporality to be solved by enfolding individuals into a transcendent history of their own construction. The postmodern move is to assert the construction of many histories or narrations as opposed to a singular metanarrative. Posthuman discourse amplifies this disintegration by fixating on self-transformation that enables individuals to survive and flourish for longer periods of time.

The natural ethic and the freedom to obey outlined above promote a counter form of discourse, challenging both the rationale and the efficacy of the posthuman project of self-transformation. This is accomplished by recovering the categories of the good and the eternal that frame the necessary and the temporal, in turn bestowing finitude with normative content and meaning. In this respect, sin may be characterized as a distorted response to necessity and temporality. Since all individual and corporate acts intending to prolong survival prove ultimately futile, finitude is perceived as nothing other than threat. Hence the strategy of Babel to build a tower reaching heaven, for in the end its builders will become something more akin to infinite gods than finite humans. The strategy is doomed to fail, however, because the resulting product is merely a simulacrum of the eternal Good.

The Christian alternative to Babel is the incarnation. In Christ, the Word made mortal flesh, the gulf separating the necessary and the temporal from the good and the eternal is bridged by a reconciler. But there is surely more to this story than the birth and life of a god-man, for otherwise Babel's strategy would be made plausible, given the infusion of an embodied divine presence. The reconciler is crucified, however, and his subsequent resurrection vindicating the order of creation does *not* entail eliminating suffering and death. Since the realms of necessity and temporality have been vindicated but not displaced, mortality and natality are ineluctable facts and normative principles that the natural ethic seeks to instantiate, affirm, and order. It is the fate of finitude inherent to a vindicated creation that Christians must come to love. Any effort to ignore these facts and norms through extensive modification of individuals and the human species is simply to revisit the failed late modern and postmodern attempts to transform necessity into goodness by ignoring the eternal Good, thereby exchanging natural and historical necessity for the necessity of the transformative imperative. Or in theological terms, treating aging as a disease to be cured by dramatically increasing longevity or pursuing virtual immortality is reasserting the Pelagian heresy of perfectibility against the orthodox Pauline and Augustinian insistence on the priority of grace.

The culminating episode of the incarnation, however, is not Easter but Ascension Day. If this were not the case, then the Pelagian strategy would be preferable, for Christ would be a goal to be pursued rather than a redeemer to be embraced. It is the risen *and exalted* Christ through which the good and the eternal delineates and redeems the necessary and the temporal. It is this eschatological hope that enables Christians to consent to finite limitations, for through the gift of the Spirit they have received the freedom to obey the constraints of their finitude, because these limitations have already been vindicated, redeemed, and taken up into the eternal life of God. To love the fate imposed by the temporal constraints of necessity is thereby also to love creation's eternal destiny in its exalted Lord and Savior. To love anything less is to love partial and incomplete goods rather than *the* Good. In this respect, even if the best dreams of contemporary medical technologists come true, the best they can offer is a kind of subjective immortality, never eternity.

If the preceding inquiry is at all correct, or at least compatible with Christian precepts, then is there any insight to be gained regarding the shape of a bioethics that claims to be Christian? Allow me to suggest one implication: in coming to regard aging as a disease that can be treated and presumably cured, contemporary medicine has entered the domain of posthuman discourse. The transformation of human beings per se, however, is not the issue at stake. Christians share with posthumanists the belief that humans should be transformed. The contention is over the purpose and source of this transformation.

If the incarnation is to have any significant import for how Christians pursue this dispute, they must begin with the insistence that the finitude entailed in our status as embodied creatures is not merely an unfortunate limit to be overcome but defines and delineates the normative shape and pattern of human life within the dictates of temporal necessity. Why else would the Word who became flesh share in the most common experiences of birth and death? And why else the need for a crucified reconciler, resurrected savior, and exalted lord as the instrument of creation's vindication and redemption? If flesh is ultimately not important, then Gnosticism, in both its late modern and postmodern manifestations, offers a far more appealing salvific story: escape, flee, or otherwise overcome any and all biological limitations.

Since I have already dismissed objections based on biological essentialism and inherent human dignity, why do I bother to assign any normative significance to finitude? My appeal is to the theological conviction that the vindication of created order resulting in the resurrection of Jesus Christ is not manifested in the erasure of finite limits. The necessity of mortality and natality, and their subsequent temporal and moral ordering, is not voided by Easter Sunday. But neither does this vindication imply that such necessity and its temporal ordering have been set in stone. There is the accompanying eschatological hope that creation and its creatures will be transformed in the fullness of time, in the parousia. The ascended Christ does not leave behind a creation locked in a holding pattern.

The natural ethic derived from creation's vindication insists that a line can and should be drawn regarding the extent to which humans, both individually and collectively, transform themselves. Yet in our obedient freedom it is a line that will need to be redrawn in response to the development of more efficacious technologies and medical practices. The placement, however, is not arbitrary. Medicine should remain an intergenerational practice of ordering biological and social reproduction instead of becoming a technological quest for virtual immortality. Consequently, Christians should also resist the rhetoric of treating aging as a disease to be prevented, treated, and cured, for it distorts healthcare into brokering longevity rather than providing healing and care. The rhetoric disguises a consuming survival ethic that too easily justifies the commodification of embryos, eugenic manipulation of offspring, and unfettered euthanasia. It is for the sake of loving and protecting these most vulnerable neighbors that Christians must endeavor to place the onus on advocates of self-transformation rather than on its opponents. The question to be answered is "why" instead of "why not." This placement of the burden is justified, because if the preservation of given boundaries is in principle disparaged in advance, then the necessity of survival in tandem with the transformative imperative has already resolved the dispute in favor of a posthuman future. If there are no lines or boundaries worth preserving, then there is no created order that has been vindicated.

Christians, however, are not perpetual border guards. In freedom, lines can be redrawn as warranted. Yet the freedom invoked here is not one of negating finite limits, for what is at stake is coming to terms with the normative status of the *flesh* that the Word became to reconcile the necessary and the temporal with the good and the eternal. It is, therefore, the freedom of obedience that conforms believers to Christ, and it is this conformation rather than the imperative of self-transformation that suggests when and where new lines, if and when needed, should be drawn. This is admittedly an ambiguous freedom that should inspire spirited argument, thoughtful deliberation, and faithful discernment both among Christians and with their secular interlocutors. It is a worthwhile debate to enter, especially for those who wish to invoke a bioethics that claims to be Christian.

7

Revitalizing Medicine

Empowering Natality vs. Fearing Mortality

One of the great accomplishments of modern medicine is arguably the gains that have been made in extending longevity. Throughout the twentieth century average life expectancy increased dramatically across the globe, a trend being continued in the twenty-first century with the notable exceptions of sub-Saharan Africa and Russia. For the first time in history, it now seems "normal" that a person should live a long, healthy, and active life.

Although the trend line is still moving up, it has started to plateau. The steep increase in longevity was achieved initially through relatively simple things such as improved nutrition and sanitation, declining infant mortality through better prenatal and postnatal care, and the development of inoculations and antibiotics. More modest gains have been achieved with the use of new diagnostic techniques and therapies for treating such life-threatening conditions as cancer and heart disease.

But the momentum in extending longevity is slowing, and many scientists believe that 120–125 years is the outside boundary that cannot be crossed. The Hayflick limit is evidently ironclad and absolute. Medical advances may be able to bring more individuals closer to this boundary, but few, if any, will cross over. Regardless of how proficient physicians may become in extending the lives of their patients, biology insists that death will still have the final word.

There are some dissident scientists, however, that believe this boundary can be pushed farther out. As has been discussed in previous chapters, with the advent of stem cell research and regenerative medicine, and with anticipated developments in biotechnology, nanotechnology, and bionics, there is talk of extending human life spans to perhaps 150 years, or even 175 or 200 years.[1] The more optimistic voices speak in terms of millennia rather than decades or centuries. The most adventurous prognosticators boldly assert that, contrary to Leonard Hayflick, the biological boundary is not absolute and can be crossed; immortality is within our grasp once we develop the appropriate technologies.[2]

It is tempting to dismiss these predictions as little more than wishful thinking. After all, despite the billons of dollars invested in life prolongation research, no significant advances have yet been made, except for some lucky mice and nematodes who lived three times as long as their less fortunate peers. The prospect of living longer seems at best a distant dream, and at worst an idle fantasy. It would be a mistake, however, to curtly dismiss the possibility of extreme longevity as little more than science fiction masquerading as science. In the first place, although research to date has been disappointing, this does not eliminate the possibility of dramatic breakthroughs in the future. If anticipated breakthroughs are forthcoming, then it behooves us to start thinking about the subsequent moral, social, economic, and political implications—if Social Security and Medicare are in a mess now, imagine a world populated by sesquicentennials.

Secondly, and more importantly, the rhetoric surrounding life extension research is prompting us, again as noted in previous chapters, to treat aging as if it were a disease. With the development of more effective therapies and preventive measures, many more people are living long and active lives. The image of a pensioner dozing in a rocking chair is not the poster child of AARP. Rather, that organization promotes and supports cheerful and energetic seniors spending their lengthening golden years endlessly playing golf in Florida. Although some of the more immodest predictions regarding life prolongation may never prove true, the research is nonetheless enabling more people to live independent and active lives as they grow older. The trick is not only to live longer, but to maintain youthful strength and vigor.

It may be asked: what is wrong with living a long, healthy, and active life? The short answer is: nothing at all. Contrary to Leon Kass's objection that extended longevity would result inevitably in tedious boredom,[3] I think I could find plenty of worthwhile things to do if I could live to be a 120 or more. The issue at hand is not living longer per se, but rather, what sense are we to make of this puzzling perception of aging as a disease that can be treated and perhaps cured?

Many of the champions of regenerative medicine and life prolongation research refer to aging and death with such terms as "annoyance," "irrational encumbrance," and "tragedy." Yet how has it come to be that morbidity and mortality are somehow inimical to human flourishing when they have been very much a normal part of our history as a species? Many people have grown old, and as far as we know, no one has ever lived forever. It would appear that a natural and healthy fear of death has been malformed and personified into a foe that must be vanquished. It is doubtful that medicine can win a war against aging and death, but how would such an unremitting struggle shape (or misshape) healthcare, and how would humans come to regard themselves as beings dedicated to overcoming their mortality?

The Beginning and End of Life

Hannah Arendt can help us think about these questions. She asserts that natality and mortality—birth and death—are the defining features of the human condition.[4] They are the brackets within which humans shape and live out their lives. Their work, hopes, and aspirations have meaning only within a temporal and finite structure that has a beginning and an end. Indeed, without a beginning and an end, the word *life* has no real meaning.[5] In confronting death, humans encounter mortality as the "only reliable law of life" that inevitably carries "everything human to ruin and destruction."[6] According to

Arendt, in death individuals face the prospect of their disappearance from the earth and its history; their permanent separation from the families, friends, and communities that shaped and sustained them.[7] In death we face the prospect of the utter and complete annihilation of who we are and what we aspire to become.

When we become fixated on mortality, is it not a natural reaction to find some way to fight against, overcome, or otherwise cheat this cruel fate? And is not some type of quest for immortality a rational strategy in this respect?[8] That we try to achieve a kind of immortal presence among subsequent generations through things we produce or legacies we leave? Through offspring a genetic inheritance is passed on to future generations. The ancient Romans tried to build an immortal empire,[9] while late moderns attempt to construct an everlasting history.[10] Although individuals grow old and die, lineages, empires, and histories purportedly live on forever.

May we not say that our current fascination with employing medicine to extend longevity reflects a similar obsession with mortality? Ironically, our success in extending longevity has fixed our attention more relentlessly upon death. The principal difference between the ancients and late moderns is that the latter's gaze is cast simultaneously toward individuals *and* corporate structures. As late moderns we not only want to establish an immortal legacy through a lineage, an empire, or history, but to live our individual lives for as long as possible, even striving to achieve personal immortality. Pursuing this twofold strategy requires a triumph of the will in which we construct our world and ourselves in the image of what we want it and ourselves to be, and the power to achieve these goals is seen most vividly in our growing use of various technologies.[11] Consequently, we construct our children, political communities, and histories as artifacts of a corporate will, and we turn to medicine to construct ourselves individually as self-made artifacts.

This twofold strategy for conquering death, however, is comprised of diametrically opposite goals, leading to inevitable tensions, conflicts, and contradictions. If, on the one hand, individuals are dedicated to reengineering themselves to live as long as possible, perhaps even achieving personal immortality, there is no compelling reason why they should invest their time and energy in projects that are designed to outlive them. Why should individuals invest themselves in building an immortal lineage, empire, or history if the goal is to live forever? Such tasks simply detract attention from achieving the objective of personal survival. The more time and money I spend on my daughter, for instance, the less I have to spend on myself. This is especially a waste of time and money if the goal is to develop medical care that wards off the ravages of aging so that I can remain independent rather than depending on my daughter (or anyone else) to care for me as I grow older.

On the other hand, if we are dedicated to constructing lineages, empires, and histories that are intended to outlive us, extending the survival of most individuals, much less achieving personal immortality, is irrelevant and may even prove inimical. Individuals are expected to sacrifice their interests for the sake of the future. Investing in personal longevity wastes resources that could be better applied to these more expansive tasks. If, for example, I invest heavily in improving my cardiovascular system but fall victim to Alzheimer's disease and linger on for decades, I no longer contribute to but detract from the task of building the collective future in which I am supposed to be immortalized. It would be better for all concerned if I would go sooner with heart disease than later with dementia.

This conflict, which may be characterized, respectively, between *selfishness* and *altruism* is admittedly little more than a caricature of the more complex relationship between these seemingly contradictory behaviors. A key tenet of evolutionary psychology, for instance, contends that the two are intricately related; that altruism presupposes and is dependent upon selfishness. The reason I am inclined to sacrifice my own desires and spend my limited financial resources on my daughter is that she carries my genes. Through her I will live on after I die. In this respect, it is in my self-interest to be altruistic. It is only in my fear of death that I am motivated to invest in my daughter's future.

Although proponents of evolutionary psychology overstate their case, they nonetheless offer the salient insight that morality cannot be casually separated from biology. If in fact evolutionary psychology is correct in this regard, might our medical war against aging and death create some unwanted and troubling consequences? Again risking oversimplification, the dilemma can be stated as follows: if I am dedicated to living for as long as possible, and perhaps forever, will I not lose my motivation to invest in my daughter's future, or even to produce and raise offspring? Conversely, if altruistic behavior is grounded in selfishness, should we take the risk of waging a war against aging and death if it lessens, or even removes, the fear of death as an underlying motivation?

The more pronounced implications of this dilemma can be seen with greater clarity by focusing on some ethical issues at the beginning and end of life. At the beginning of life, great advances have been made in prenatal and neonatal care. Many infants who would ordinarily not have survived or would have suffered chronic conditions due to poor prenatal care or premature birth are now able to live happy and productive lives. With the assistance of various reproductive technologies, many infertile couples are able to have children. To the casual observer, it would appear that late modernity is a child-friendly, even pro-natalist, culture.

Appearances, however, can be deceiving. An increasing number of individuals are choosing to remain childless, a goal that is assisted by various contraceptive techniques and easy access to abortion. More effective screening and testing (e.g., amniocentesis and preimplantation genetic diagnosis) are enabling parents to prevent the birth of children with deleterious conditions or other unwanted characteristics, to select desirable traits (e.g., sex), and perhaps in the future to produce so-called designer babies. Not only have these techniques resulted in the destruction of many fetuses and embryos, but with the prospect of embryonic stem cell research and therapeutic cloning, prenatal life may come to be perceived as a biological resource or commodity that can be exploited in developing better healthcare. Again, to the casual observer, it would appear that late modernity is a culture that is at best indifferent to children, and at worst hostile.

These contradictions are played out with an alarming symmetry at the end of life. Tremendous strides have been made in treating, and in some cases curing, a growing range of diseases that a few decades ago were tantamount to a death sentence. The popular media, for example, talk about surviving cancer as a real possibility instead of a desperate hope. It is generally presumed that with a combination of a healthy lifestyle and proper medical care, virtually anyone can live a long and active life. Moreover, improved pain medication and palliative care have made the prospect of an "easy passing" more readily available. To the casual observer, it would appear that late moderns are fashioning a culture that cherishes life and are developing a healthcare system devoted to its prolongation.

Yet again, appearances can be deceiving. Under the banner of "quality of life," death is also promoted as a means of exercising the right to control one's fate. When one has determined that the quality of one's life has reached such a low ebb that continued existence is no longer desirable, then one should be able to control the time and means of one's death. Hence the growing public tolerance, if not acceptance, of euthanasia and assisted suicide. Moreover, exercising this personal choice to "die with dignity" has also created a subtle expectation that the dying should not be assisted in lingering too long, becoming a burden on others. Again, to the casual observer, it would appear that late moderns have little tolerance for morbidity, and little patience for caring for the dying.

How may we account for these apparent contradictions at the beginning and end of life? The strategies summarized above are quite rational within the following conceptual scheme: although some promising initial forays in the war against aging and death have been launched, late moderns are not placing all their eggs in this basket but hedging their bets. Declining birth rates tacitly acknowledge that in striving to live long and active lives, children are both an encumbrance upon one's lifestyle and a drain on financial resources. Offspring are now more an option than a necessity, as reflected in the puzzling perception of children as a means of their parents' self-fulfillment. Hence the growing recourse to and anticipation of "quality control" techniques that help parents obtain the kind of children they want.

Yet there is also a grudging admission that offspring remain a necessity should the war against aging go badly. As people grow older, they may still need their children, not to care for them directly but to be productive taxpayers. The late modern phenomenon of lengthy retirements coupled with declining birthrates is a recipe for long-term financial disaster. A shrinking cohort of young workers simply cannot support an expanding collection of unproductive pensioners. Consequently, some European countries are now paying women or providing other economic incentives to have children, and

China has admitted that around 2050 a shrinking population will displace overpopulation as its principal social and political problem. In short, children are becoming both an artifact of their parents' will and an insurance policy for the future.

A similar hedging strategy is also at play at the end of life. There is heavy investment in medical treatments and technologies that are designed to prolong the lives of individuals while also maximizing their mobility and independence. But if medicine should fail to deliver the proffered goods, then individuals want to exercise the options of euthanasia or suicide should the quality of their lives become burdensome or undesirable. Even if the war against aging and death should be lost, humans can at least have a final, defiant gesture by choosing when and how they die. In this respect, our deaths are also artifacts of our will.

These seemingly contradictory strategies being employed at the beginning and end of life become more explicable when the war against aging and death being presently undertaken is placed within the larger late modern project of asserting greater mastery over nature and human nature.[12] Late moderns have come to believe that they must construct their world and themselves in an image of what they want to become in order to be more human and humane; their lives and their future are largely what they make of them. To be human has become virtually synonymous with being the master of one's own destiny. To assert greater control over the beginning and end of life is to exert greater mastery over life itself. In this respect, death remains the final, and most elusive, object of this mastery.

If this chapter were ended on this note, the reader might be rather despondent, for the world described above is the one envisioned by that troubled and troubling philosopher Friedrich Nietzsche—a world of restless and anxious nihilists. Fortunately, I have concentrated and expanded upon only half of Arendt's depiction of the human condition, namely, that of mortality. To complete the picture we need to turn our attention to her account of natality. Arendt insists that fixating on death means that anything genuinely human ends in ruin and destruction. Humans become trapped in Nietzsche's eternal recurrence of the same, for there is no purpose or direction to human life over time.[13] Some kind of principle is needed to disrupt this deadly pattern, and Arendt proposes *natality* as a promising candidate. By "natality," she means something more than physical birth, although this act symbolizes the disruptive power to break the pattern of mortality. Each new baby embodies a hope of new possibilities; something new is started and is thereby also renewing.

More broadly, natality entails the acknowledgment that there are fundamental limits inherent to what it means to be human. In other words, to be human is necessarily to be finite and temporal. It is only within the imposition of these given limits that humans are liberated to break the pattern of death and be genuinely creative or, better, *pro*creative in the sense that they create social and political structures that are greater than themselves, enabling human generations to flourish over time. Yet it must be stressed that natality can be embraced only by accepting, while also refusing to fixate on, mortality. The creative and renewing potential of birth can be effective only by consenting to the inevitability and necessity of death.

Withholding such consent in favor of a longing for personal immortality distorts the moral ordering of human life, because it removes the limits that give morality its meaning and purpose. This is the trap, Arendt notes, that the immortals or gods of ancient Greek mythology fell into. The pantheon of the gods was populated by beings that could point to their birth but did not face an impending death; they lived deathless lives of endless time. In the absence of death, the ensuing void was filled with an insatiable appetite for power and mastery. The immortals were objects of fear, but certainly not models to be emulated. More often than not they were vain, capricious, and cruel. The gods magnified every conceivable human vice while belittling virtue. The quest for immortality, Arendt suggests, leads inevitably to moral decay, for what is lacking is any "rule of an eternal God."[14]

To consent to, rather than war against, the inevitability and necessity of mortality redirects attention back to natality, and in redirecting our gaze we discover the common life that binds people together over time. The renewal that natality offers provides the social and political bonds that embody, in Arendt's words, "what we have in common not only with those who live with us, but also with those who were here before us and with those who will come after us."[15] It is also through the possibilities engendered by natality that moral precepts and virtues such as self-denial and regard for others are preserved, enabling humans to live together peaceably, especially across generational divides.[16] Consequently, natality rather than mortality—birth instead of death—should provide the principal metaphor for ordering our common, political life.[17]

Arendt's argument is highly suggestive, and the remainder of this chapter explores some avenues for revitalizing medicine by turning our attention away from mortality and toward natality. A preliminary step of preparing some theological soil must be taken, however, in which her philosophical argument may be planted. Such theological soil is needed for, although Arendt has correctly identified the fateful late modern fascination with death, she cannot quite bring herself to identify an eternal Good or God that would redirect our attention toward birth. The best she can offer is a politics based on justice that endures and improves over time as the highest good that humans can attain. This is admittedly a worthwhile goal that should not be easily dismissed or despised, but on its own it can be neither attained nor sustained. Her project depends upon a strength of will that is too weak to stay the course. The temptation to become fixated on mortality is too compelling to be resisted on our own accord. Rather, Christians believe that the highest good is fellowship with God through one's life in Christ, which is in turn a life of grace instead of the will to power.

The Gift and Loan of Life

In preparing this theological soil, it should be admitted that although the medical war against aging is motivated by the fear of death, this fear is not irrational or cowardly. As St. Paul acknowledged, death is the final enemy,[18] and when confronting any formidable enemy, fear is a normal and healthy response. It should also be admitted that the desire to live a long and active life is neither wicked nor perverse. The issue at hand is *how* the old enemy death should be confronted, and *how* the good desire of living long and active lives should be pursued. In thinking about this "how," Christians may start with the incarnation. In Jesus Christ God became a human being; the Word was made flesh.[19] The creator became one with his creatures, complete with their mortality and finitude. As attested in scripture and affirmed by the creeds, Jesus was born of Mary and died on the cross. In these acts we may say there is an affirmation of both natality and mortality. The gospel, however, does not end with Good Friday. Death does not have the final word, for in resurrecting Jesus Christ from the dead, life is renewed within the eternal life of the Triune God. Easter Sunday is the ultimate act of natality.

Death is faced, then, as a powerful but already defeated enemy. Like all such enemies, it should be respected while not granting it finality, for in death we are raised with Christ into the eternal life of God. This is not an easy moral and religious stance to take, for death is real and cannot be cheated. Jesus did not avoid death, and neither will his followers. Death remains an enemy that should never be warmly embraced, but it should be struggled against on God's terms and not ours. This is why regarding aging as a disease that can be treated, and perhaps cured, is not only futile, but also misdirected. Waging a war against aging and death is misguided because there is nothing inherently unnatural, irrational, inconvenient, tragic, or unjust that humans grow old and die. Aging is simply not a disease, but a sign of our status as temporal and finite creatures. Christ did not come into the world to rescue humans from their finitude, but to welcome them to eternal fellowship with their Creator.

In treating aging as if it were a disease, a fateful mistake is made by confusing immortality with eternity, for the two words are not synonymous. In brief, immortality entails a beginning but no end, whereas eternity has no beginning or end. This is not to invoke a fine semantic distinction, for the difference is important and has grave practical implications. The quest for immortality requires a world of endless time. Is this a bad world? Yes! It is a world of frenetic and constant work without rest, because there is no end or purpose to one's labor. It is a world of ceaseless and often pointless construction, deconstruction, and reconstruction, a world in which births, deaths, and lives are reduced to artifacts of frenzied willing. It is a world devoid of the good, and filled with values of one's own making. It is a world populated by frustrated souls in search of a perfection that will always elude them, for the goal is a projected fabrication that is itself always changing, somewhat like Alice's Wonderland, in which you may have jam yesterday or tomorrow but never today. In short, it is Nietzsche's world of the will to power that has gone beyond good or evil, and therefore a world predicated on raw power instead of love.

What a quest for endless time fails to recognize is that finite mortal creatures, such as humans, require a beginning and an end if their lives are to have meaning, direction, and purpose. The realms of natural necessity and human history are bracketed by eternity; the eternal serves as bookends to the story of human existence. Christ is the Alpha and the Omega of creation and its creatures precisely because he is also the eternal Word of God. It is also the eternal that is the source of the true and the good that are revealed in the incarnation, and it is in Christ that we gain inklings of what the good and the true entail, and we are called to conform our lives accordingly. Ironically, to strive relentlessly after more and ultimately endless time is to become fixated upon death.

As St. Augustine taught, a properly ordered life is one that desires to know and to be embraced by the good and the true, a life that seeks fellowship with the eternal God. He likens this fellowship to the eighth day of creation, an eternal Sabbath rest.[20] Any other desire can only frustrate and disappoint, for our hearts remain restless until they find their rest in God.[21] It is properly God alone that should be the object and goal of what we ultimately love and desire. To reemphasize, the desire to live a long and active life is not an evil or wicked desire, but if it is pursued for the sole purpose of extending longevity within a quest for endless time, it corrupts this otherwise good desire. Again as St. Augustine recognized, the problem of sin, more often than not, is not that we desire bad things but that we desire good things badly.[22]

May we not say, then, that trying to live for as long as possible by any available means is a disordered desire because it means we desire our own survival more than we desire God? Moreover, does it not also mean that we fear our own deaths more than we fear or love God? If true, then a promising possibility presents itself: what would medical care look like if rather than seeing it as a means of prolonging life, we perceived it as a means of preparing ourselves for eternity? Or to use Arendt's metaphors, how would medicine be practiced if the fixation upon mortality were displaced by attending to natality, particularly at the beginning and end of life?

In the first place, we would be better equipped to resist the temptation to regard birth and death as artifacts of our own creation. Rather, we would see life as a gift that properly is not subject to our mastery and control. The concept of life as a gift has been developed in some detail by such theologians as Karl Barth,[23] Gilbert Meilaender,[24] and John Kilner,[25] and I can only summarize briefly the more salient features of their portrayals. Starkly put: our lives are not our own; they belong to God. Life is not a product we produce or own, but a gift that is entrusted to us, and we are to care for and use this gift in accordance with God's expectations and commands. This sentiment is captured most vividly in the sacrament of baptism.[26] When parents present their child to be baptized, they simultaneously accept the divine charge to love, cherish, and protect this life that has been entrusted to their care, and they in turn commend their child back to the love, grace, and care of God in Christ as the origin and end of life itself. The child is not, in Meilaender's apt but chilling phrase, the outcome of a reproductive project, but the beneficiary and recipient of their fellowship as wife and husband. In this respect, parents are not so much producers or creators of new life as they are trusted stewards or custodians.

Consequently, an orientation toward natality as opposed to mortality rejects the notion of children as artifacts. On the one hand, although being a parent may prove rewarding, a child is not properly a means of parental self-fulfillment. If this were the case, then a child could not embody the kind of hope and possibility that Arendt envisions. It is precisely because a child is *both* like and unlike her or his parents that genuine fellowship between generations is established and honored. If a child is merely an avenue of personal fulfillment, then she or he is like any other instrument that is used in constructing one's lifestyle: an object exhibiting the will of its creator. It is only in recognizing the similarity and otherness of a child that mortal bonds are forged while the fateful drift into mortality is broken.

On the other hand, although children should care for their parents as they grow older, they are not insurance policies. Placing one's hope for the future upon any child (save one) is to impose a burden no child can bear. Again, if this were the case, then a child would be little more than the sum total of parental aspirations. Such a prospect is bound to prove barren for both child and parent,

143

for the former is not the slave of the latter. God, and God alone, is the proper object of hope. It is in placing our hope in God that we are freed to consent to death, and in such freedom children are empowered to both receive *and* subsequently pass on the gift of life. Counterintuitively, it is in consenting to the necessity and inevitability of death that each generation is free to turn its attention toward natality and away from mortality.

What would it mean for healthcare at the beginning of life to be oriented toward promoting natality? Three suggestions: first and foremost, providing easily accessible prenatal, neonatal, and pediatric healthcare. It makes little sense to affirm procreation but remain indifferent to the health of children.

Second, policies should be strengthened or enacted that support parents in fulfilling their duties and obligations. It makes little sense to perceive children as embodying future possibilities if they are not given the resources to fulfill this potential. Having said this, however, it must be stressed that this responsibility is properly lodged with parents instead of the state or other social service agencies, which should play a supportive rather than a leading role. In this respect, tax and legal codes, as well as other economic incentives and support mechanisms that protect and empower marriage, family, and educational choice should be regarded as public health issues.

Third, greater respect for prenatal life needs to be exhibited. Like many others, I have grown weary over the endless and acrimonious debates over abortion, embryonic stem cell research, and therapeutic cloning. At present, however, an adequate political consensus does not exist to offer anything approaching a definitive resolution. Nonetheless, it is incumbent upon Christians to keep pressing these issues, if for no other reason than to raise public awareness. How the most vulnerable members of the human species are treated discloses a lot about the moral convictions of the civil community, and where it places its hope and confidence for the future. Casually destroying and exploiting prenatal life for either the sake of convenience or their potential to develop medical treatments should, at the very least, give the public some pause. If we are to be genuinely oriented toward natality, can we continue to neglect and prey upon the future?

An orientation toward natality as opposed to mortality will also reject any notion of death as an artifact. Life is a gift that is entrusted to our care, but *not* our keeping. The gift is also a loan with a foreclosure date, and the life given by God also returns to God. Surrendering this gift and loan back to its rightful owner does not diminish St. Paul's teaching that death remains the final enemy, but in the current crusade against aging, there is often a failure to resist this enemy properly. To use a crude analogy, we are tempted either to wage a fruitless struggle, to grasp tightly to the loan for too long, or to capitulate too early, surrendering the loan before it is due.

A long and desperate, though ultimately fruitless, struggle against death has been made possible by recent medical advances designed to prolong life. The blessing, however, has also become a curse. The modern image of death is a patient lingering in a hospital attached to various tubes and monitors. A death at home in the company of friends and family has been exchanged for a sterile room surrounded by machines and healthcare professionals. This is the kind death late moderns wish to avoid, for it seemingly strips them of their dignity. They cannot recite with much enthusiasm a petition from the Great Litany that reads, "from dying suddenly and unprepared, good Lord deliver us," for they rightfully fear the prospect of dying in pieces.[27] What this failed strategy of prolonging life at any cost fails to recognize is that there is a subtle yet profound difference between extending life and delaying death. Given this prospect, the second temptation of succumbing too early is understandable. When the quality of one's life has deteriorated to an unacceptable level, one should be allowed and assisted to relieve the burden or put an end to the lingering life of an unconscious person. Is this not a preferable option to dying in pieces, an act of mercy in the face of prolonged pain and suffering? What this seemingly compassionate strategy fails to recognize, however, is that there is a subtle yet profound difference between allowing a person to die and hastening death.

In waging a war against aging, both of these acts are defiant gestures against an adversary that cannot yet be vanquished. One can either wage a desperate but heroic struggle to the bitter end, or end it on one's own terms at a time of one's choosing. Both options purportedly provide the satisfaction of somehow cheating death, but in fact they cheat life. In attempting to dictate how and when we die, we implicitly deny the sovereignty of God who is the Lord of life. But let us also admit that given the present circumstances of

145

late modernity, these options are not irrational or perverse. Again, it is a case of disordered desire. There is nothing wrong in desiring a good death, which is the literal meaning of *euthanasia,* but how that good end is achieved is what is at stake.

Since our lives are not our own, then neither are our deaths. Rather, humans, as creatures created by God, are called to be stewards of life, ordering their lives in obedience to God's will and commands. Exercising such stewardship is a challenging and perilous enterprise, for as sinners humans more often than not fail to discern correctly what the obedient ordering of their lives means and requires of them, particularly when their lives are coming to an end. An admittedly imperfect principle that can guide our moral deliberation is that we seek to prolong life in ways that do not merely delay death, and we also allow death to occur while not hastening its arrival. Consequently, Christians must steadfastly resist policies that allow or promote assisted suicide and euthanasia. Although these are certainly live options, they are not acts that affirm life. Yet resistance must always be tempered with humility and compassion, avoiding the acrimony and recriminations that often characterize the state of contemporary moral and political debate. Barth's teaching on suicide is helpful in this regard. He insists that although suicide is wrong, the person committing it should not be condemned, for we can never know what God's final command might have been, and neither are we in a position to dictate the limits of God's mercy and forgiveness.[28] In resisting assisted suicide and euthanasia, we encounter the perennial task of hating the sin while loving sinners. In this respect, Christians should spend far more time bearing witness to what a genuinely good death means and entails, rather than denouncing what they oppose.

Modeling a good death is an urgent task, for practically how do we allow death to occur without either hastening or delaying it? How should people die in ways that are life-affirming? In this respect, Paul Ramsey's observation is apt that the problem at hand is not the fear of death, but the fear of dying alone and abandoned.[29] Christians should take the lead in promoting and assisting greater access to advance directives and durable power of attorney, improved palliative care and hospice services. Most importantly, they should strive to maintain and strengthen the bonds of fellowship with the dying to ensure that they are not abandoned. Especially within the church, greater attention needs to be directed toward how the dying are included within the life and ministry of the community that gathers in Christ's name.

To conclude, again there is nothing wrong with living a long and active life; it is a blessing that should inspire praise and thanksgiving. Yet it is not surviving, of living a long life per se that makes this blessing a good gift. It is rather the extended opportunity to worship and serve Christ, to love God and neighbor that makes this gift good. The attempt to wage war against aging and death, however, is tantamount to refusing this gift, for in fixating on the avoidance of death, we forget how to affirm life. Ironically, medicine is being used to promote a culture of death rather than life. Arendt's emphasis on natality offers a potentially helpful metaphor for revitalizing medicine and redirecting its underlying culture. Yet Christians need to make the stronger claim that medicine should not be used to wage a war against death, for in the fullness of time it has already been defeated. They may affirm with St. Paul: "Where, O death, is your victory? Where, O death, is your sting?"[30] This is not merely a pious platitude, but an assurance and a starting point for being good stewards of the gift of life that has been entrusted to our care.

8

The Future of the Human Species

If a number of pundits are correct, as late moderns we have already taken some initial steps toward creating a posthuman future.[1] The goal of this project is nothing less than the perfection of the human species. Specifically, as noted in previous chapters, human performance will be enhanced and longevity extended through anticipated advances in pharmacology, biotechnology, and bionics. Drugs, for example, can lessen the need for sleep, genetic engineering will slow the aging process, artificial limbs will enhance strength and agility, and brain implants will enhance the speed of interacting with computers. The cyborg becomes the next stage of human evolution.[2] Some visionaries foresee a day when with the aid of artificial intelligence and robotics endless lives might be achieved. The underlying binary information constituting one's personality would be uploaded into a computer and then downloaded into robotic bodies or virtual reality programs. With sufficient and reliable memory storage, the process could, in principle, be repeated indefinitely, thereby achieving virtual immortality.[3] In the posthuman future, humans become self-perfected artifacts by blurring, if not eliminating, the line separating the natural from the artificial.[4]

The promise of the posthuman project is the creation of beings that live healthy, productive, and happy lives, and most importantly, beings that live for a very long time, perhaps forever. The ultimate promise is immortality. The accompanying peril, however, is that the cost is exorbitant. The price of perfecting humankind is its destruction, for in becoming posthuman, humans cease being human. The peril of the posthuman project, in short, is that its optimism disguises an underlying death wish for the human species.

One might be tempted to object that any worry about this peril is misplaced. The peril presupposes a promise that is far from certain. Few, if any, of the requisite technological advances have yet been achieved, and the likelihood of dramatic breakthroughs any time soon is slim at best. A so-called posthuman future is based on science fiction, not science. Consequently, time should not be wasted worrying about a peril that might, but probably will never, present itself.

There are two reasons why this temptation should be resisted. First, even in the absence of the technical advances and breakthroughs that would be required, we nonetheless must come to terms with the extent to which technology is shaping the fabric and trajectories of contemporary life. As Martin Heidegger and others have observed, technology has become the ontology of late modernity, our mode of being in the world by mastering and reshaping it in an image of what we want the world to become.[5] In large part, humans now live, and move, and have their being within fabricated environments that have become their natural habitats. It is through technology that they increasingly express who they are and what they aspire to become. This is not a mere acknowledgment of the ubiquitous presence of machines and gadgets within the fabric of daily life, but that in increasingly turning to medicine to control their behavior, regulate their biological processes, and repair and sculpt their bodies, humans are literally coming to embody a technological age. Focusing on the prospect of a posthuman future, which is admittedly far from certain, nonetheless helps us to come to terms with where, as late moderns, we are placing our hope and confidence. To ponder the prospect of becoming posthuman requires that we also ask the question of what it means to be human, and any answer we offer cannot avoid the question of technology in general, and medicine in particular.

Second, even if most, if not all, of the more immodest expectations—such as immortality—never come true, posthuman discourse is nevertheless shaping a vision of the future, and thereby derivatively our moral imagination. How the future is envisioned informs current moral convictions and conduct, and it does not matter how improbable, strange, or fantastic such a vision might appear to be in exerting such influence. Whether, for example, I believe that I will live a long and sickly life or a short but robust one goes a long way in shaping how I spend my time and money in the meantime. Whether or not either scenario is likely is largely irrelevant, for I become a certain kind of person in reaction to what I believe the future entails; if I believe that my life will be short and sweet, I become a free-spending bohemian. In a similar vein, if we believe, either implicitly or explicitly, that we can and should exert greater mastery over nature and human nature, that belief goes a long way in shaping what we do and how we treat each other in the present. In this respect, N. Katherine Hayles is correct in asserting, "People become posthuman because they think they are posthuman."[6] Such posthuman thinking should, at the very least, prompt some deliberation on its good or ill effects in forming our moral imagination, particularly in light of growing technological power and potential for further development.

Deadly Perfection

A promising avenue for pursuing such deliberation is suggested by the early work of the President's Council on Bioethics in which its members discussed Nathaniel Hawthorne's short story "The Birthmark."[7] Although the exercise was derided by many reporters and bioethicists as a waste of time, it reflected the insight of its chairman, Leon Kass, that fiction is often quite perceptive in revealing fundamental convictions, hopes, and aspirations, offering a fruitful starting point for moral deliberation and discernment.

"The Birthmark" is a tale about a brilliant scientist who marries a stunningly beautiful woman. Her appearance is perfect in every regard except for a tiny birthmark on her cheek. The scientist becomes obsessed with this tiny, barely perceptible flaw, and he concocts various potions to remove it. Over time his efforts succeed. The birthmark disappears, but only at the moment that his wife dies;

151

the medicine can cure only by killing. In Hawthorne's words: "As the last crimson tint of the birthmark—that sole token of human imperfection—faded from her cheek, the parting breath of the now perfect woman passed into the atmosphere . . ."

Hawthorne offers a sober warning: the quest for perfection leads to a deadly destination. The cost of removing the flaw is a corpse. The applicability of this story to the posthuman project is obvious: humans must first be killed in order to perfect them. The extinction of the human species is certainly one possible consequence that should give some pause in assessing the prospect of a posthuman future, but it is not the most likely outcome. Rather, technological reconstruction may eventually produce a new species that is deemed to be superior, but to what extent these new beings can be said to be perfect raises questions: by what standard of perfection is this judgment made, and what are the costs of attaining this perfect state? In other words, the underlying and unacknowledged death wish driving the posthuman project is not an overt desire to exterminate humankind, but an ill-advised attempt to strip away the vulnerability and imperfections that enable humans to be human and humane. It is not the death of humankind, but its humanity, that is at stake. We can begin to unfold this more subtle endeavor by taking a look at another short story by Hawthorne.

In "Rappaccini's Daughter," the reader encounters the highly acclaimed physician Dr. Rappaccini, his lovely daughter, Beatrice, and a young medical student, Giovanni, who is living in the guest room. One of the chief features of the villa is a large garden that is filled with exotic plants, each one of them highly poisonous. The slightest contact is lethal, and even a quick sniff of their aroma causes illness. To stroll through this garden, one must keep his distance. Yet Beatrice is seen embracing the plants and breathing deeply of their fragrance. As the story unfolds we learn that since her birth her father has been slowly giving her increased dosages of the poisons he has been extracting from the garden. The effect has been to make her immune and invulnerable to any disease.

Giovanni and Beatrice fall in love. Yet through their courtship they never embrace, kiss, or hold hands, for like the plants from the garden Beatrice is lethal to the touch. In the meantime, Dr. Rappaccini has also been administering the same procedure to Giovanni without his knowledge. The father wants to create an intimate companion for his lonely daughter. When Giovanni learns that he too is being made invulnerable by becoming poisonous, he is appalled. A rival of Dr. Rappaccini on the medical faculty gives Giovanni an antidote that purportedly will make both him and Beatrice normal again. The couple makes a pact, but Beatrice insists that she take the antidote first, and she dies.

This sad tale offers three lessons that may guide an assessment of the posthuman project: first, the cost of invulnerability is high. Dr. Rappaccini has purportedly achieved his goal of preventing Beatrice from contracting any deadly disease. She will be spared needless pain and suffering, and given a power and invincibility that few enjoy in confronting a cruel world. Yet it will be an isolated life, devoid of any physical contact. She can neither touch nor be touched by others, for she is literally poisonous to anyone other than herself. Her life will also be devoid of any intimate and lasting relationships, a crushing fate, as her father recognizes in his desperate attempt to transform Giovanni into a suitable, and equally poisonous, companion. Beatrice's invulnerability has made her something less than human. May we not say, then, that in attempting to transform humankind into a superior species humans run the risk of the death of their humanity?

Second, there is no going back. When Beatrice finally finds someone with whom she can purportedly share her life with fully, Giovanni is appalled by what he is becoming. Out of her love she agrees to forsake her invulnerability and return with her lover to a natural state where together they may risk a vulnerable embrace. The attempt, however, proves futile and deadly, for her transformation had been complete and irreversible. In Hawthorne's haunting words: "To Beatrice—so powerfully had her earthly part been wrought upon by Rappaccini's skill—*as poison had been life*, so the powerful antidote was death."[8] May we not say, then, that once we travel very far down the posthuman path, it may prove difficult, if not impossible, to turn back?

Third, even if the promise is achieved, the consequences are ambiguous and uncertain. Because of Beatrice's death, we never know how the life of a poisonous couple might unfold. Would they be able to fully embrace, or would their respective lives prove too toxic to interlock in any meaningful sense? Moreover, is there a significant difference between the embrace of two invulnerable beings and that of vulnerable creatures? Would they be able to have offspring? If so, would their children share with them a life of poison, or would they be unable to touch what they have begotten until Rappaccini's skill worked its transformation once again? May we not say, then, that even if the posthuman promise of a superior species is achieved, we do not know what will become of the human spirit and soul, and thereby whether or not these new beings will prove to be truly superior?

Hawthorne's stories—written in the early nineteenth century—help to expose the posthuman project for what it really is, namely, a religious movement, and not a new or original one at that. The central posthuman precept may be summarized as follows: finitude and mortality represent the dire plight of the human condition. It is irrational and unfair that humans suffer, grow old, and die. In response, posthumanists offer the salvation of human transformation and perfection, culminating in virtual immortality.

Hawthorne reminds us that this is an old complaint. Few, if any, of our ancestors warmly embraced their mortal limits. There is also nothing novel about the proffered solution. Hawthorne's plants and potions are simply exchanged for genetic engineering, miniaturization, silicon chips, and binary code. Consequently, it should not be surprising if Christians in particular hear some familiar notes in this posthuman tune, for they have encountered similar themes before in what they identified as false religious beliefs. In more formal terms, posthuman discourse is based largely on philosophical or theological precepts about nature, human nature, and human destiny that are derived from what may be described as heretical doctrines. There are three prominent strands that we may focus upon in this chapter.

We may conveniently call the first strand *nihilism*. Nihilism is a modern philosophical orientation that posits that the world is devoid of any purpose or meaning. Consequently, there are no objective moral standards, only a subjective will to power. Humans assert this will over inanimate objects such as stones and cars, animate things such as plants or animals, or other people such as children and students. For late moderns, technology is the principal means that is used to assert this power. Minerals are transformed into steel to build cars, genetic engineering is used to produce better plants and animals, and drugs and psychological techniques are developed to control the behavior of children and students. The world, our lives, and the lives of others are artifacts that we construct, and the future is largely what we make of it and will it to be.

Friedrich Nietzsche has become closely associated with this philosophical orientation. It should be noted, however, that although he accurately describes the nihilism of late modernity in all its lurid details, he does not commend it. Indeed, he is alarmed by its destructive potential. Nihilists can too easily conclude that in a world where there is nothing noble to will, it is better to will nothing at all; a despair leading to unspeakable violence. This is why he places his hope in the *Übermensch*, or Overman, a superior being that will rise above the fray and provide some meaning and purpose in a meaningless and purposeless world. Perhaps Nietzsche's hope can become real in the transformation of the human into the posthuman. Why not direct the otherwise directionless will to power toward the constructive goal of creating and perfecting a superior species?

This leads to the second strand that we may call *Pelagianism*. Pelagianism is a theological doctrine that is derived from that arch-heretic Pelagius, who caught the wrath of St. Augustine. The central tenet of Pelagianism is that Adam's fall did not corrupt human nature. Subsequent generations are not infected by original sin. They possess an innate ability to know the difference between right and wrong and may choose the former without God's assistance. Salvation resides within each human heart and does not depend upon the initiative of a divine redeemer. It is ultimately human action, not God's, that counts. Consequently, humans can will themselves to be good; they can even will themselves to be perfect. And they can use their technological ingenuity to help them achieve this perfection.

In their more sober moments nihilists and Pelagians recognize, however, that there are severe constraints that must be overcome in asserting the will to power and the will to perfection. This leads to the third strand, which we may call *Manichaeism*. Manichaeism is a dualistic teaching that draws a sharp divide between the physical body and what may be variously described as an immaterial spirit, soul, or will. It is this immaterial essence that defines who we are and what we aspire to be. Unfortunately, this essence is trapped

155

within a weak and fragile body that constrains the will to power and perfection. No matter how much in my youth I may have willed myself to be a Major League pitcher, I did not have the body that would enable me to perfect a blazing fastball and killer curve. No matter how much we may will ourselves to live, eventually our bodies fail us and we die. What Manichaeans in every age long for is to be rescued, to be saved from their bodies. The promise of virtual immortality, a life free of embodied limitations, then, is also the promise of salvation.

Given these formative strands, Christians are rightfully skeptical of the posthuman project, for it represents a corruption of their faith. Christians may concede that the patterns and trajectories of human life are to a large extent a matter of the will, and such willing certainly entails gaining and asserting various kinds of power. In the absence of such willful power, civil communities, for instance, could not exist. What Christians do not affirm is that power itself is a proper object to be willed; rather, power is a means of achieving that which is willed.

What is the highest or greatest good that humans should will? The short answer is, of course, God. If humans direct their will toward any lesser goods, their subsequent desires and lives become misdirected, disordered, or, to use a word that is falling out of favor, sinful. The consequences of sin are grave. When the will is misaligned, for example, the attempts to fulfill the great command to love God and neighbor ends up as love of self, which we expect God and our neighbors to honor and support. The will to power, in short, is little more than a thin justification for narcissistic self-indulgence. The great moral task of any generation is not the triumph of the self-oriented will, but to align what is willed in obedience to God's will.

Knowing God's will, much less aligning oneself to it in faithful obedience, is, admittedly, no easy task. The ways of God are inscrutable and unsearchable. Contrary to Pelagius and his latter-day disciples, humans do not have it within them to know the mind and will of God and therefore cannot know how to will and perfect the good. The great danger of Pelagianism is its underlying arrogance that if we just keep trying harder, we will somehow achieve perfection, but the endeavor itself is a fantasy. In his book *The Perfectibility of Man*, John Passmore examines the unhappy legacy of Pelagius within the history of Western civilization.[9] One of the more prominent problems is that the ideal perfection to be achieved is a moving target, subject to changing social, cultural, and political circumstances. At various times contemplation, virtue, reason, politics, revolution, and eugenic purification have been lifted up as models of the perfect life that should be pursued. As Passmore notes, all of these projects failed miserably, and he adds the grim observation that whenever the idea of perfection—whatever it may happen to be—has seized public attention, there is increased intolerance directed against those judged to be incapable or unwilling to attain the proffered goal.

What Pelagians of every age fail to recognize is that what little humans know about what perfection might mean is not a result of their will to power, but is a gift of grace. We cannot will ourselves to be perfect; we can only admit that in our imperfection we have been embraced and upheld by God in Christ. Receiving this gift of grace should not only inspire a response of gratitude, but should also make us mindful of the limits that are inherent to us as finite creatures that are in great need of this gift. Consequently, humans are not called to live lives in which they are constantly trying harder to obtain a perfection that cannot be obtained, but to live grace-filled lives of confession, repentance, and amendment of life. Or, in other words, to live lives as creatures of God who accept their finitude and mortality as a blessing rather than a curse.

It is in respect to bodily limitations that humans encounter with great intensity the inherent limitations of their creaturely status. Humans are not only creatures; they are *embodied* creatures. As such they are also finite and mortal beings, and therefore subject to bodily limitations. Humans cannot do everything they want, and they cannot live forever, since their bodies are unable to withstand the ravages of time and natural necessity. Posthumanists can only respond to these limits with a Manichaean disgust and disdain for the body, because it is the chief obstacle preventing them from successfully achieving the will to power and perfection.

This means, however, that the posthuman project is predicated upon a fundamental contradiction: for humans to achieve their full potential, they must destroy their bodies, but in doing so they destroy the very thing that makes them human. Despite all the rhetoric about enhancing the performance of bodily functions, the posthuman project is driven by a hatred and loathing of the body. Extending longevity and improving physical and mental functions is merely an interim strategy until such time that virtual immortality is achieved, liberating humans from their weak and fragile bodies. Yet is not this high-tech Manichean dream tantamount, as Paul Ramsey once observed, to a suicidal death wish for the human species?[10]

It is embodiment that decisively separates posthumanists and Christians, for their assessments of what it means to be human lead to differing beliefs about salvation. Unlike posthumanists, Christians have never believed that humans are creatures who unfortunately happen to have bodies. Rather, to invoke Ramsey's imagery again, humans are inextricably embodied souls *and* ensouled bodies.[11] Consequently, humans are not saved from their bodies, but it is as embodied creatures that they are claimed, redeemed, and renewed by God. This is why Christians are not driven by a death wish, for as St. Paul reminds them, death remains the final enemy that is not to be fraternized with, much less warmly embraced.[12] Yet humans consent to their mortal and finite limits because they are *creatures* who have been created in the image and likeness of God, and it is as embodied creatures that they love, serve, and are in fellowship with God. The finite and mortal limits that posthumanists loathe and hate are received by Christians as a blessing, for these limits enable them to be the creatures God intends them to be. To despise the constraints and fragility of embodiment is to also despise the work of the Creator.

Graceful Destiny

If the preceding portrayal of the posthuman project as a religious movement incorporating the formative strands of nihilism, Pelagianism, and Manichaeism is correct, then there are good reasons why Christians should not only be skeptical but should also oppose it. There is, to be sure, a cornucopia of rich resources within their theological tradition they may draw upon in making their case against the underlying false and heretical beliefs. It is not enough, however, to be against something; simply opposing the posthuman project will not do. A constructive proposal regarding what Christians affirm must also be offered. If Christians are to help shape contemporary culture—particularly in a late modern setting in which the posthuman message proves attractive, if not seductive—then they must offer an alternative and compelling vision, a counter theological discourse. In the remainder of this chapter, some of the basic contours of this theological discourse are sketched out by focusing on two anthropological questions: "What does it mean to be human?" and "What is the destiny of the human species?"[13]

In addressing these questions, Christians begin with the simple affirmation that anthropology *is* Christology. What this admittedly inelegant phrase is meant to convey is that "Jesus Christ" is the short answer to both questions. We turn to Christ to learn what being human means, and to catch a glimpse of our destiny as a species. In making this anthropological claim, it is important to keep in mind that in fixing our gaze upon Christ, we are also encountering the Triune God. The God who is in Christ the Redeemer is the same God who is the Creator and Sustainer, the God who is also Father and Holy Spirit. Being attentive to Christ is also attending to God in his fullness, the eternal One who is the origin and end of creation, and thereby the One who gives creation and its creatures their direction and purpose. It is only in this respect that Christ's otherwise immodest claim that he is the Alpha and the Omega is explicable and illuminating.[14] What might we find by fixing our gaze on Jesus Christ? An exhaustive answer is beyond the scope of a single chapter, or the career of any single theologian for that matter. More modestly, allow me to suggest three things to look for.

First: the *incarnation*. The centerpiece of the gospel is the extraordinary claim that in Jesus Christ God became a human being. The Word became flesh and dwelt among us full of grace and truth.[15] We may say, then, that in the incarnation the necessity of finitude and mortality, of human limitations more broadly, is affirmed rather than condemned. It is important to stress, however, that in emptying himself and taking on human likeness, Christ also shares the human condition, complete with its suffering, pain, and death.[16] In his life and ministry Jesus does not avoid or escape the constraints of finitude but embraces them, and in doing so he reconfirms a divine blessing. The life and lives of God's creatures, however vulnerable, fragile, and imperfect they might be, are nonetheless good precisely

159

because they have been created and blessed by God, a doxology that is sung, in a manner of speaking, in the incarnation. Most importantly, Jesus does not cheat death. Again, it is important to stress that Jesus *dies* on the cross; the events of Good Friday produce a corpse that is placed in a tomb. How could it be otherwise if indeed the Word had become mortal flesh?

But death is not the final word, which leads to the second item to look for in Jesus Christ: the *resurrection*. Drawing upon the work of Oliver O'Donovan,[17] Jesus Christ's resurrection from the dead vindicates Jesus's life and ministry. Moreover, since God is incarnate in human life, the vindication extends to all of creation. Because humans were not "allowed to uncreate what God created,"[18] there is a created order to be discerned because it has been vindicated by its Creator. The resurrection of Jesus Christ, in short, entails the resurrection of humankind and with it the renewal of creation.

What exactly does this vindication and renewal of creation entail? First and foremost, it discloses a *created order* that provides an objective standard and teleological order against which human desires are both judged and conformed. This objectivity is seen in what was described in a previous chapter as the "natural ethic."[19] Contrary to the posthuman project, the moral life is not a constructed artifact that is designed to enable the will to power and perfection. Rather, Christ's resurrection discloses in greater clarity that human life and lives should be oriented toward certain moral structures and relationships that are inherent to the order of creation. Women and men, for instance, are drawn to each other not merely to reproduce in perpetuating the species, but also to form bonds of affection between themselves and with their offspring. The generations are literally linked together through a natural chain of mutual and sacrificial love.

The teleological order of creation can be seen in social structures that order and promote these bonds of love and affection. Marriage, for example, is oriented not only toward enriching love, affection, and mutuality between spouses, but also toward promoting mutual and self-sacrificial bonds between parents and children. It is through one generation surrendering itself to the following one that human life and lives flourish over time. What is especially noteworthy is that the embodied character of human life is absolutely crucial in obtaining these goods of marriage and family, for it is only as embodied creatures that humans can interact and love one another in any meaningful sense.[20] The physical, finite, and temporal limitations that posthumanists decry are the very features that provide the rich texture of human life beyond the bare minimum of natural necessity. It is the creaturely finitude and mortality affirmed in the incarnation and vindicated in the resurrection that the posthuman project wishes to annihilate.

A vindicated and renewed creation is also genuinely liberating, because it provides the foundation of *obedient freedom*.[21] Through Christ's resurrection we simultaneously look back to the origin of creation in Christ, *and* to its destiny in Christ. This Januslike vision leads to the third and final theological feature, namely, *eschatology*, or the destiny of the human species. In the absence of this dual orientation, humans become enslaved to a false perception of nature in which any inkling of a natural moral order is perceived as a threat. Consequently, finitude and mortality are inimical to their survival and flourishing; they are threats to human welfare that must be vanquished. Hence the posthuman project of transforming humans into an invulnerable and immortal species. The project, however, is based on the false assumption that freedom is expanded by overcoming all finite and temporal limits. Only the invulnerable and immortal being is purportedly free.

The posthuman project is actually enslaving, for it leads to an inability to be obedient, and as such disabled beings humans disfigure their proper dominion over and stewardship of creation into domination and mastery of nature and human nature. By looking to creation's destiny in Christ, however, these so-called threats are revealed as given and necessary limits that define and order human life and lives. Humans are free to love their fate, because it has already been taken up into the eternal life and fellowship of their Creator and Redeemer. In this respect, true freedom is a gift of the Spirit that frees humans to be obedient to the definitive limits that shape their lives as finite and mortal creatures. In short, we are free only by being limited. To return to the previous example, we are free to be married only when we limit our intimacy exclusively to one other person; we are free to be parents only when we constrain our self-interests for the benefit of our descendants.

More broadly, Christ's resurrection from the dead discloses the destiny of creation and its creatures. There is a future trajectory revealed in the resurrection of the incarnate one, signifying its destiny in the exalted Christ. Such a future orientation inspires an ordering of human life that is teleological rather than perfectionist. Creation and its creatures will be transformed in the fullness of time, and humans will contribute to this transformation. Posthumanists are correct in this regard, but they have been seized by a half-truth that in its incompleteness proves destructive and dangerous. For our transformation is shaped by Christ, and not by our attempts to overcome the finite and mortal limits of a created order. The Creator who has vindicated creation will also redeem it fully in the fullness of time. In this respect, a life of obedient freedom is also a life of preparation for eternal and timeless fellowship with God instead of a quest for immortality and endless time, a consenting to God's will being done on earth rather than the triumph of our will to power and perfection. In this respect humans look forward to this completion, this divine perfection, when even the created and natural goods of marriage and family, for instance, are no longer necessary, for the roles of wife, husband, parent, and child are transformed into the eternal fellowship of sisterhood and brotherhood in Christ.

If the preceding analysis is correct, then we are offered sharply contrasting options regarding the future of the human species. On the one hand, the posthuman project, with its will to power and perfection, and hatred of the body, offers the construction of a superior and immortal species. On the other hand, there is the Christian offer of eternal fellowship with God through a life of obedient conformity to God's will, but it is not a future that offers any escape from finitude, suffering, and death. We must be careful about which destiny we choose, taking precautions that our choice is not the result of inattention or naïveté. The practical decisions that are made today in regard to research and development in such areas as medicine, biotechnology, nanotechnology, bionics, and the like will not be inconsequential for the future. We must choose wisely, for contrary to the spirit of our age, the future is not something we construct; rather, we are enveloped and enfolded in the particular destiny that we choose.

In his essay "Thinking about Technology," George Grant provides an insightful meditation on this question of destiny.[22] He contends that we perceive technology as a collection of neutral instruments that we use in ways that we choose. Like any other technology, we use a computer, for instance, to read an e-book, keep a ledger, or surf the Internet. The computer simply does not impose upon its user the ways it should be used.[23] Grant believes that this reassuring image of technological neutrality is misleading. Of course the computer, like any technology, imposes the ways it should be used upon its users; otherwise, it could not be used for the purposes for which it was designed. Reading an e-book, for instance, is not the same as reading a printed book. More broadly, we cannot easily pick and choose how technologies are used, because they incorporate certain values and purposes that cannot be separated. Any project of technological development enfolds and shapes its users in its accompanying logic and destiny. As Grant has observed: "To put the matter crudely: when we represent technology to ourselves through its own common sense we think of ourselves as picking and choosing in a supermarket, rather than within the analogy of the package deal. We have bought a package deal of far more fundamental novelness than simply a set of instruments under our control. It is a destiny which enfolds us in its own conceptions of instrumentality, neutrality and purposiveness."[24] Technological development inevitably transforms, for good or ill, those who are undertaking the project in the first place, and it transforms who they think they are, and what they aspire to become.

If Grant is right, then we should be wary of the posthuman project, for once we initiate a process of transforming the human species, we become enveloped in a destiny that takes on a life of its own, one that is not subject to our control. Like any destiny, it imposes itself, and its imposition has stark and unavoidable moral consequences. Grant offers salient and sobering advice in regard to the posthuman project, that once we start down the road of transforming ourselves it will be difficult to slow the momentum, much less change or reverse course. The danger is that such a momentum might carry humankind toward a destiny whose consequences are both unforeseen and unwanted. We become locked into a new set of circumstances that we can neither change nor control, for there is no going back. To return to the computer as an example, when the Internet was introduced with the great promise of easy and instant access to abundant information, who foresaw that it would also become a cesspool of pornography, child predators, and financial theft and fraud? Yet are there any serious proposals for tearing up or even staying off the information highway?

To a large extent, Grant reinforces the messages of Hawthorne's stories: be careful how you go about creating beautiful, invulnerable, and perfect people, for the project may enfold you in a deadly destiny. This is an especially poignant warning, for it reminds us that the evil we commit is more often than not the result of a myopic moral vision rather than a wicked heart. Dr. Rappaccini loved his daughter, but he cared, in Hawthorne's words, "infinitely more for science than for mankind"; and as the brilliant scientist in "The Birthmark" looked upon his now perfectly beautiful but dead wife, Hawthorne notes that "he failed to look beyond the shadowy scope of time, and, living once for all in eternity, to find the perfect future in the present."

Is not finding the perfect future in the present the moral and religious challenge that confronts us in the prospect of a posthuman future? And is this not a particularly difficult challenge in a late modern world that has largely forgotten how and where to look? This difficulty stems largely from a prevalent cultural conceit regarding creativity. Late moderns have come to believe that they are a creative people who have the power to create their world, themselves, and their future. They are a creative people who are masters of their own fate, so why bother to look in the present when one's gaze should be fixed permanently toward the future?

Yet arguably, as creatures humans create nothing, for that is a task that is reserved exclusively by and for *the* Creator. We make things, but that does not make us creative. Art best exemplifies the difference between making and creating. Artists make such things as paintings and sculptures. Skilled artists make beautiful objects, but they do not create beauty. Rather, their art reveals the beautiful, drawing the beholder into a realm that is beyond either the work of art or the artist. In this respect, art at its best is iconic, for it points beyond itself to the Creator of beauty. When we encounter good art, we look in and through it to the source of its beauty. Art is revelatory of something greater than itself and is debased when it serves only to glorify and immortalize the so-called creativity of the artist.

In a similar manner, may we not say that the posthuman project is the attempt to *create* a superior species as the triumph of the will to power over nature and human nature and thereby draws attention to its own ingenuity and creativity? And in recreating ourselves as self-made artifacts of the will to perfection, are not posthumanists trying to glorify and immortalize their own skill and creativity? Yet the end result will not be a superior and perfected species, but a debased humanity, producing beings who have forgotten that they are creatures and not creators. In short, posthumans can point to nothing greater than themselves, beings that have drunk deeply from the poisonous wells of Manichaeism, Pelagianism, and nihilism.

As we take our first, tentative steps toward a posthuman future, it is not enough for Christians to be critics only. They must also embody and bear witness to an alternative future, a perfect future that in Christ is already in the present. In this respect, they must insist that technology generally should be developed and used in iconic ways that reveal the work of the Creator who is the source of all that is good, true, and beautiful. In particular, Christians must strive to recover and preserve medicine as a healing art that discloses Jesus Christ as the true nature and destiny of the human species.

9

Creation, Creatures, and Creativity

The Word and the Final Word

A few years ago NewScientist.com posted an interview with three artists.[1] This is not a typical Web site for staying current with artistic trends, but these are not typical artists. They work closely with scientists employing biotechnology to create works of art. Laura Cinti, for instance, creates transgenic cactus that is able to grow human hair. Since cacti are "not known for their beauty," and the spines on their "phallic stems" exude antisexuality, adding the human hair gene transforms the cactus into a "sexual symbol." Her purpose was never to transform cacti into beautiful objects, but to create a "perversion" that "resonates with the cultural climate surrounding genetic engineering," and in doing so her "Cactus Project brings that perversion into focus and reverses it. The cactus with its hairs coming out is showing all the desires, all the signs of sexuality. It doesn't want to be trapped. It wants to be released. The desire is to enter the world as a species from a mythical landscape." Responses to Cinti's artwork range from angry scientists to enthralled bald men.

Oron Catts uses pig bone marrow stem cells to create pig wings. Again, the purpose is neither to create an object of beauty nor to make flying pigs. Rather he wants to draw attention to artistic creations "that are partly alive and partly constructed," which "raise huge ethical and epistemological questions which people haven't begun to think about." The ambiguity of these questions is reflected in the fact that it is difficult to discern whether these wings are more similar to those of angels or vampires.

Marta de Menezes alters a butterfly while it is developing in a cocoon so that it emerges with one wing much larger than the other. Her purpose for doing so is twofold: on the one hand, she wants to use biotechnology to master a form of manipulation that she likens to a painting technique. On the other hand, she wants to raise, as vividly as possible, the issue of what is or what is not natural. By altering the symmetry of butterfly wings, she has created something that is seemingly not natural. Yet "everything in the butterfly is natural because I didn't add anything: I just changed the pattern. But that is not natural. It makes you wonder exactly what 'natural' is." Her next project is to "make the stripes of zebra fish vertical instead of horizontal so that they look more like zebras."

The reason for summarizing the work of these artists is *not* to enter the old debate of what is and what is not art. Rather, the purpose is to pose the broader issue of creation and creativity: what does it mean to create and to be creative? In general, late moderns value creativity, and if we are willing to suspend aesthetic or moral judgments, we can readily admit that these artists have created some novel things. That admission, however, discloses the extent to which the formative categories of nature, science, technology, and art have collapsed into a single act that enables individuals to create and to be creative. These works of art symbolize late modernity's attempt to blur, if not erase, the borders separating the organic from the inorganic, the natural from artifice. Moreover, we are at a loss to judge whether these artistic creations reflect goodness, beauty, truth, or loveliness, because there are no clear standards to determine whether such creativity is good, beautiful, true, or lovely. Consequently, to be creative is to produce something, anything, so our response to a hairy cactus, pig wings, or a genetically altered butterfly is not to determine whether these artistic expressions are good or bad, beautiful or ugly, but only to give reasons why we either like or dislike them.

It may seem perplexing that the topic of this chapter has been included in a book on bioethics, since it concentrates on technology in general, and information technology (IT) in particular. There are two reasons, however, why it is important to ponder this topic. First, IT is to date the most fully developed attempt at mastering nature and human nature. This is not simply because of the ubiquitous presence of IT in our daily lives. Rather, cybernetics as the underlying science of this technology reinforces the perception that *all* borders are tenuous and permeable. While sitting at our computers, do we not have the sense that we are manipulators and creators of patterned information in which boundaries are fluid rather than fixed? This perception will be amplified as IT is incorporated within a larger network of anticipated developments in artificial intelligence (AI), artificial life (AL), robotics, nanotechnology, and biotechnology. Moreover, IT is a conceptually underlying or foundational technology for late modern medicine and healthcare. Various diagnostic and therapeutic techniques are predicated upon the ability to transform organic matter and processes into binary code.

Second, engineering language is one of the most effective ways of mastering nature and human nature. Through language we learn how to perceive and understand the world. It is also through language that we express who we are and what the meaning of our lives might be in this world. It is through words that both the beholder and beheld are formed and expressed. Without language there can be no culture that could be called human. Consequently, it is significant whether or not language can be reduced to information that is easily manipulated and reconfigured, thereby implying that the media used is unimportant. Since one task of moral theology is to form human life and lives, it cannot ignore the issue of language. The very theological language employed will form the resulting life of faith. Is the task at hand to conform believers to a way of life mandated by Jesus Christ, or to enable them to creatively fashion their lives of faith? It is one thing, for instance, to form Christians as stewards of a creation entrusted to their care, and quite another to form them as so-called cocreators.

In the remainder of this chapter, I explore some selected implications regarding the broad relationship between creation and creativity through three meditations: 1) from word to icon; 2) from creatures to cocreators; and 3) *telos* and *logos*. I use the term *meditation* because what follow are not carefully developed arguments. I am frankly unable to conceive a plausible conceptual scheme for coming to terms with the emerging range of new technologies, particularly in respect to medicine and healthcare, that seem destined to transform human life and lives in the future. What it means to live in a world where time and place are increasingly fluid, where nature and artifice are coalescing into a single reality, is beyond my ability to describe with much precision or assess with much insight. Hence, these meditations are provisional and speculative.

From Word to Icon

The Word creates. In the opening chapter of the Bible, God speaks the world into existence. Through six days of successive utterances, God creates a world that did not previously exist. It is important to note that it is through speech, rather than painting or sculpting, that creation is brought into being, for a spoken word demands a reply, even if it is one of silence. When one thinks silently, one is responding to one's own interrogation; we literally talk to ourselves.[2] Consequently, God is seemingly answering his own question when at the end of each day he pronounces that what he has spoken into being is good, and on the final day of Sabbath rest, creation is said to be very good. It is through the Word that God creates, and that Word is simultaneously descriptive and evaluative; creation is both real and good.

It is through words that as creatures humans attempt to discern and describe the creation that the Word created. This is no easy undertaking, and it is doubtful whether language will ever be up to the task, for we are replying to the question posed to us by the very Word that created us. This is why theology and philosophy at their best employ tentative and approximate vocabularies, for they are engaging through their respective languages the question of truth that cannot be known, much less mastered, in its entirety. It is the Word that forms and measures our words.

Consequently, this is also why theology and philosophy are at their best when they are pursuing wisdom and endeavoring to speak wisely.

In doing so, theologians and philosophers conform their speech to the Word's created order. It is also through wisdom (*Sophia*) that God speaks creation into being. There is, so to speak, a grammar and syntax of the created order that demands to be honored.[3] Theological and philosophical attempts to discern wisdom and speak wisely, however, will always and necessarily be imperfect and incomplete, because our knowledge of creation is also limited and imprecise. We cannot simply gaze at creation and discern its created order. Wisdom does not stand naked before us but reveals herself on her own terms, thereby concealing as much, if not more, than she discloses. Hence, all theological and philosophical attempts at discerning wisdom confront a deafening reply of silence in response to our questions posed to the Word, and given the awkward nature of that silence, theologians and philosophers too often succumb to the temptation of divorcing reason from reverence.

This separation, however, cannot produce knowledge that is wise, for it settles for facts rather than truth. As a result, language can be descriptive, but not evaluative. We may say that creation *is* and what *it* is, but not that it is *good*. Moreover, descriptive discourse requires no reply. The objects we behold simply *are,* and the questions posed only by the beholder are those of *what* and not *why*. Consequently, we need not wait for the object we behold to disclose itself; we strip it down to the facts we are striving to discover and master. This preference for factual certainty over ambiguous wisdom makes our lives less anxious, for we need not concern ourselves with ordering our speech, and thereby our lives, in line with the truthful order of the Word that can only vex us with its elusive refusal to ever be fully known, much less mastered. Or such was the promise of the Enlightenment project.

As late moderns we are coming to believe that this project has largely failed. There are no facts to be discovered and described, only interpretations located in particular perspectives. At best, we exchange information, and it is up to the recipient, not the sender, to determine the meaning and value of the data in question. E-mail has become a fitting metaphor for the mutation of language, in both its written and oral forms, into the creation, dissemination, and assessment of data. Each day one must determine what is spam, what is trivial and what is important with no standard other than

171

the value that is assigned to each item. The advert for cheap Viagra, for instance, may be of greater value to someone on a given day than the lengthy missive from a boring relative. In turn, we send out batches of messages not knowing how they will be evaluated and valued by the recipients. An attempt at humor, for example, may be interpreted as an insult. Since all we have is information to exchange and interpret, language cannot be ordered to truth, wisdom, or even facts, but is an instrument to shape and express oneself, and a tool for forming the objects and inhabitants of our constructed worlds in the image of what we would like them to be. In short, there is no Word that creates, only words to be used creatively. Or as T. S. Eliot expressed it:

> Where is the life we have lost in living?
> Where is the wisdom we have lost in knowledge?
> Where is the knowledge we have lost in information?[4]

With the descent of language from wisdom to knowledge to information in mind, we turn our attention to the icon. An icon is a visual portrayal aiding one's contemplation of a greater reality or mystery. It is this religious connotation and setting that dictate its purpose and use. One does not properly look at an icon but sees through it; it is, therefore, a revelatory instrument. When it becomes an object of contemplation in its own right, it ceases to be an icon, becoming a piece of art displayed in a museum, or a commodity to be bought and sold.

Christians have had a long and troubled relationship with icons. I am not well versed in the intricacies of the debates over iconography, but I understand that the principal issue at stake is how we prevent pictorial images of the faith, or those inspired by faith, from becoming idolatrous. The most extreme solution is to avoid any such aesthetic temptation altogether, as exemplified in the stark architecture and conspicuous absence of ornamentation in Puritan churches. According to Jacques Ellul, Christians have good reason to be deeply suspicious, because the icon moves us away from the realm of speech to that of the seductive and dangerous realm of sight.[5] It is in the former realm that the Word is revealed, while in the latter the same Word becomes distorted and humiliated by the image. To

172

portray the world in terms of images is to disfigure its created order, because it can be properly discerned only through discourse, not visual representation. A movie, for instance, can never do justice to a good novel or its author. Sight prompts us to desire and possess the objects we see in the world, unlike speech, which is not a commodity to be owned. Indeed, sight is the underlying rationale of technology, accounting for late modernity's insatiable appetite for consumer items in tandem with its ongoing attempt to master nature and human nature.

Although Ellul overstates the dichotomy between word and image, his analysis nonetheless helps to identify what underlies a rapacious consumerism and will to mastery, especially as exemplified in two late modern distortions of the icon. First, there are the icons that help one to navigate the computer. In one respect, these images retain some semblance of a proper icon in that they are a means to an end. Rather than seeing through these icons, however, one clicks them to open a window or program. In these realms the user does not encounter a greater reality or mystery but is enabled to be creative and to consume the creative efforts of others. With a series of clicks and keyboard entries I can, for instance, compose an essay, revise a spreadsheet, draw a picture, or compile a photo album. I can also surf the Web, collecting and revising information in line with my particular interests and tastes. I enter fluid realms where information is nearly instantaneously created, shared, and altered at my beck and call. Again with a few clicks, I can transform the home page of my favorite Web site into *my* home page.

The net result is the illusion of greater control that by extension makes one more creative. Unlike writing, where we must first collect our thoughts before putting pen to paper, keyboard composing allows our thoughts to flow freely. We are thereby liberated to more freely and creatively express ourselves, for cutting and pasting is much easier than writing a second or third draft.[6] Indeed, in principle there are never a rough and a final draft, but only a document in process. Moreover, this technology enables the blending of narrative and image into a seamless creation, in turn transforming our understanding of what constitutes knowledge and how it is acquired. Knowledge becomes a commodity to be produced and consumed, and it is through a greater range of customized choices offered that

173

we are afforded greater control of creating and expressing who we are through the commodities we create and consume. The reason why the Internet is becoming the preferred medium for acquiring and exchanging information is not because it is necessarily easier or less time-consuming, but because of the broad range of options and sensual stimulation it offers in comparison with other media. Why should we settle for a book as the equivalent of the corner mom-and-pop shop, when we can enter a vast shopping mall of virtually limitless options?

The illusion of greater control and creativity that a larger range of options purportedly offers is amplified when we pause for a moment to consider what we are really doing with a computer. We are not creating or beholding words or images, but the visual results of manipulating script—a series of 0s and 1s—that manifests itself as words and images on a screen. It is controlling and manipulating underlying data that allows us to be creative. When we click an icon, we enter the fluid realms of cyberspace in which we perceive worlds where there are no permanent borders, and time is rendered irrelevant by making it virtual. Consequently, both the beholder and what is beheld are simply temporary patterns of information.

Second, the celebrity has become iconic. There have always been heroes that capture public attention, and at times its adulation. The late modern celebrity, however, is almost purely an artifact of commercial manufacturing and mass marketing. The body of the celebrity is sculpted, the voice amplified, and the talent enhanced. The goal, moreover, is to make the product appear ubiquitous by seizing public attention, so we are continuously assaulted with the images of celebrities on television, Web sites, and magazine covers. But they are images frozen in time. The celebrity must appear to be eternally youthful, alluring, or talented. In the late modern celebrity we also encounter an icon, but it is not one that can be either seen through or clicked. It serves more the role of an opaque idol against which our rather drab lives are measured and found wanting. Consequently, although some individuals may aspire to achieve this iconic status set before them, they will almost always fail to achieve this prized goal, despite the Herculean efforts of *American Idol* and its inevitable lesser spin-offs. Yet in principle, anyone can become a celebrity if he or she possesses the prerequisite tools for manufacturing and promoting himself or herself as such. Most importantly, we cannot judge whether such idolatry is good or bad; we may only express our like or dislike of particular idols. We can choose only either to consume or to refrain from consuming iconic commodities.

The problem with the iconic celebrity is that it cannot remain frozen in time. Despite the best plastic surgery, technological enhancements, and spin doctors money can buy, celebrities grow old; they lose their allure, and their talents fade. Unlike cyberspace, finite borders are not entirely malleable, and ultimately time cannot be made virtual. Consequently, in late modernity we face the challenge of combining the iconography of the celebrity with that of cyberspace. This is necessary if we are to more effectively overcome the finite and temporal limits that are imposed upon us as embodied creatures. If in fact we are at the early stages of endeavoring to surmount these limits, then the cyborg takes on an iconic status. The cyborg symbolizes the effective erasure of the borders separating the organic from the mechanistic, and the natural from artifice, thereby giving it greater and more creative control over time and space. This is precisely the theological and philosophical claim that such writers as Philip Hefner[7] and Donna Haraway,[8] respectively, are making, and it is worthwhile to consider why they are making it with such fervency. The following meditation offers some initial thoughts on how we might begin to come to terms with this iconic attraction by pondering what might be motivating late moderns to become cyborgs.

From Creatures to Cocreators

As humans we are creatures that have been created by a creator. As such we have been made and not begotten by God, but we nonetheless bear the image and likeness of our maker. This quality, however, does not imply equality between creator and creature. Unlike God, humans are not infinite and eternal, but finite and mortal. Yet it is also important to stress that they are *not* artifacts of divine handiwork. As humans, we are not finished products created and cherished by God in the same way as artisans cherish the crafts they construct. It is out of pure and gratuitous love that God creates. It

175

is also because of that same love that, following Simone Weil, God withdraws from creation to give it the time and space to become a proper object of love.[9] Yet this withdrawal also subjects all creatures, including humans, to the harsh demands of natural necessity. Since humans are the creatures bearing the *imago Dei*, they may use their creativity, however, to create cultures and artifacts to come to terms with and soften the rough edges of their status as finite and temporal creatures.

Cocreationists seize this capacity for human creativity, not as the means of negotiating necessity, but as *the* way of establishing fellowship with God. God created humans so that God would not be alone in the ongoing project of fashioning a creation; *creatio continua* rather than *creatio ex nihilo* should capture the theological imagination. Humans are cocreators, working with God in forming an initially incomplete creation, and shaping the life and lives of its creatures in striving to become the kind of beings they have the potential to be. These acts of cocreatorship culminate in a deeper and more expansive love between God and humankind.[10]

As late moderns we may find the image of the cocreator to be an attractive one, for we often flatter ourselves with the reassuring notion that we are asserting a progressive mastery over the quality and destiny of our lives. We are coming to believe that our lives and destinies are largely what we make of them, and our steadily growing technological power confirms this belief. Thus, our frenetic creativity is divinely sanctioned and blessed, for it is only through our creative acts that we will become the kind of creatures God wants us to be, namely, creatures with the capacity for having a progressively deeper and mutually enriching fellowship with God.

As attractive as it might be to imagine ourselves as God's cocreators, such a portrayal incorporates two problems that ultimately prove fatal to the entire proposal. The first problem involves an inadequate understanding of why God creates. Presumably, God could not tolerate a primordial and eternal loneliness, and therefore created something other than God that he could in turn genuinely love and have fellowship with. Moreover, it would take time (a very long time indeed) for a creature to emerge possessing the capacities that God desires. Through all the long and painful missteps and dead ends of evolution, at last a creature called human has emerged, capable of satisfying God's longing for fellowship.

Such a scheme presumes, however, that there is a lack or void within God that needs to be filled. This means that humans are somehow necessary for God to become complete or whole; that God cannot be fully God in the absence of cocreators. This presumption not only ignores the triune nature of God's internal life, but more significantly reflects an impoverished understanding of divine love. God purportedly creates in order to love something that in turn fulfills a need. God, therefore, has taken a risk in creating cocreators, because they may not provide the kind of reciprocal fellowship God requires to become more fully God. Such a concept of love is explicable in respect to humans. We take the risk of loving others not knowing if our initiatives will ever be reciprocated in a manner that satisfies our needs, but the cost of avoiding the risk would be the destruction of any meaningful bonds of affection and affiliation.

What this diminished understanding of divine love fails to acknowledge is that God does not love and create to satisfy a need, but rather, creation is the result of a plentitude or abundance of love. In a crude sense, creation is a gratuitous spillover from the love shared by the persons of the Trinity. God does not need creatures or their love to be fully and completely God. In the absence of a plenteous, gratuitous, and unreciprocated divine love, neither we nor God can declare that creation is good, because everything depends on the response of cocreators who may or may not respond in ways that promote the good of creation. As cocreators, the best we can say is that we live in a creation; whether or not it will prove to be good no one can say, not even God.

This task of codetermining with God the fate of creation leads to the second problem, namely, that humans attempt to bear a weight that can only be borne by God alone. If creation's destiny is not known by God, then there are no normative standards against which the acts of cocreators may be judged. Creativity itself becomes both the goal and measure of human life. In the absence of a *telos* imposed upon creation by its Creator, we cannot assess whether hairy cacti and pig wings—much less cloned human embryos and designer children—are good or bad. There is no sin to be judged, confessed, and redeemed, only misadventures to cocreate our way out of. Presumably the only sin a cocreator could commit would be refusing to be creative, for this would be tantamount to denying the sole purpose for which he or she was brought into being; it would mean rejecting the very nature of the cocreator to be a creator.

Moreover, the creative efforts of cocreators are not confined to engineering nature and culture. Their attention is also directed toward their own self-transformation. Yet in the absence of any normative *telos* informing them what humans are properly fitted for, there is in principle no end to their self-transformation. As discussed in previous chapters, with recent advances in regenerative medicine and electronic prosthetics, humans have perhaps taken the first tentative steps toward merging with their own technology. This merger will presumably fashion creatures with increased longevity and enhanced physical and cognitive abilities. Some visionaries, such as Hans Moravec[11] and Ray Kurzweil,[12] believe this process will culminate in the ability to upload consciousness into a computer and then download it into various biological, synthetic, or electronic media, thereby achieving virtual immortality. This final step will enable humans to transgress every embodied border and physical limit, as well as liberate them from the passage of time.

This envisioned future is admittedly highly speculative, for the technological developments foreseen may prove to be infeasible, but the vision itself is not without theological warrant. Would not aspiring toward casting off the finite and mortal shackles of the body be the logical course for cocreators to take? Is it not by becoming something other than human—posthuman—that cocreators become the kind of creatures that satisfies God's longing for full and complete fellowship? The willful self-transformation of humans into posthumans is not unlike Teilhard de Chardin's noosphere and Omega Point,[13] and it is the prospect of erasing all finite borders and temporal limits that enables Hefner's celebration of the cyborg's iconic status, for with the cyborg, which can be endlessly constructed and reconstructed, the boundaries separating the organic and the inorganic, and nature from artifice, have been negated.

Again, as late moderns, we might find the prospect of becoming posthuman attractive, but it is a temptation that Christians are well advised to resist. The prospect of such extensive self-transformation falls into the deadly trap of exchanging one kind of necessity for another. The desire to become posthuman is presumably motivated by overcoming natural necessity as represented by finitude, temporality, and mortality. Human beings are subjected to the pain and misery of growing old and dying. It would be good, then, if they could eliminate, or at least substantially mitigate, such pain and misery by overcoming finite limits. As discussed in previous chapters, the attempt to transform necessity into goodness is an old strategy. Hegel and Marx took this tack by using history to solve the problem. Humans could perfect their freedom from necessity through the willful creation of either Hegel's absolute state or Marx's classless society. Political or social reproduction rather than biological reproduction is the key factor in achieving a good destiny. This approach, however, does not really solve the problem of necessity and goodness but merely exchanges historical necessity for natural necessity. All sorts of pain and misery can still be inflicted and justified by the historical necessity of creating the absolute state or classless society. As Simone Weil[14] and George Grant[15] have argued, no form of necessity can ever be transformed into goodness, because they are separated by a chasm that cannot be filled in. Necessity, in both its natural and historical manifestations, is a temporal and finite realm that cannot realize the good, because goodness resides on the other, eternal side of the divide. The chasm separating the necessary and the good can be bridged only by Christ's cross as an act of pure, redemptive, and reconciling love.

Consequently, all sorts of evils can be inflicted and justified by the necessity of becoming posthuman. My unease with the notion of humans as cocreators is that a similar pattern can easily be repeated by the necessity to be creative. Yet if the prospect of becoming posthuman is to be resisted, then alternative theological ways of thinking about temporality and finitude are needed in contrast to those offered by cocreatorship.

Telos and Logos

A detailed analysis of temporality and finitude is beyond the scope of this chapter, as well as the limits of the reader's patience. In what follows I simply sketch out the lineaments of two theological

179

premises in contrast to those offered by cocreatorship. In respect to temporality, the image of the cocreator represents an attempt to solve an old theological dilemma: how is the eternal God related to a temporal creation? This dilemma arises from the central Christian claim that in Christ God became a human being and dwelt among them full of grace and truth. According to cocreationists, since Christ is both fully human and fully divine, the eternal and the temporal are joined and share a common fate. Since God in Christ has become temporally limited, the creator has also become dependent on created cocreators to shape creation into something that can be declared to be good. To use a crude analogy, because of the incarnation God's vista is more expansive than those of cocreators, but it is nonetheless temporal and limited. God cannot know the future with absolute certainty. What separates the creator from cocreators is a matter of degree, not kind.

Cocreationists are mistaken, however, in believing that the incarnation produced an ontological change in either God or humans. Ellul is correct in insisting that we cannot draw from the incarnation any universal conclusions regarding a divine human nature or a temporal divine nature.[16] In Christ, the eternal and the temporal are bridged, but the nature of neither is thereby changed. This is why Weil makes her enigmatic observation that although temporal necessity may be beautiful, it can never be good, because goodness resides in eternity. How, then, are eternity and temporality related in a way that does not negate the nature of either? Ernan McMullin offers a helpful Augustinian framework in which, despite appearances to the contrary, creation is a singular act rather than a series of sequential acts.[17] Within the eternal life of God, there is no passage of time. What humans perceive as past, present, and future is for God a singularity. Stating the matter simplistically, both the Garden of Eden and the New Jerusalem have already come and gone; the end of creation has already occurred to the same extent as its beginning. Iconic attempts at freezing time, then, are rather pointless, since time has already ceased to exist within God's eternity. This is why, parenthetically, a quest for immortality is little more than a cruel hoax, for immortals remain subject to an eternal fate that lies beyond their control. More importantly, since God already knows the end of creation, then God—and only God—can pronounce it to be good.

Since God knows the end, indeed since the end has, so to speak, already occurred within eternity, then our so-called creativity also has a given end or *telos*. Creation does not so much emerge out of its past and present as it is drawn toward its destiny in Christ. Creation is not so much the outcome of an ongoing construction project undertaken jointly by God and cocreator subcontractors but unfolds over time within God's singular act of creation. In a strict sense, we do not really create anything, but we fulfill our appointed task of exercising dominion and stewardship as revealed in God's commands or mandates regarding the proper ordering of creation. Consequently, we may affirm, along with Oliver O'Donovan, that in Christ, particularly in his resurrection from the dead, the order of creation has been vindicated.[18] This does not mean that creation does not change over time. The cocreationists are right in insisting that creation and its creatures have changed a great deal over time, but these changes are not the result of any willful alteration of the nature of creation or its creatures. The destiny of creation does not depend on the ability of cocreators to transform other creatures or themselves, for whatever transformation awaits creation and its creatures has already been completed in Christ. Thus, the *imago Dei* that humans bear is not creative license, but a sign of election: humans are the creatures God has elected to order creation toward its destiny in Christ. We may also look, then, to the goodness, truth, and loveliness revealed in the vindicated creation to gain the most important clues regarding its timely moral, social, and political ordering in the "not yet" before the fullness of time. Consequently, we may judge such things as hairy cacti and pig wings to be bad or wanting, not because they are unnatural, but because they utterly fail to disclose any signs of the good, true, and lovely origin *and* destiny of God's creation. The finite borders of the created order are admittedly permeable and transitory, but this fact alone does not give us the creative license to willfully rearrange or erase them at our pleasure.

It is apparent that the alternative theological framework for dealing with temporality and finitude sketched out above creates as many problems as it solves. It offers no definitive answers to such thorny issues as theodicy or free will, much less the maddening question of predestination. Despite these weaknesses, however, the alternative offers a more promising bulwark against the cybernetic vision of the emerging posthuman future, for it at least entertains the possibility that objects and organisms cannot be reduced to underlying information that can be manipulated. To the contrary, normative borders defining the relationship between parts and whole must be protected if the object or organism in question is not to become a mere artifact of the manipulator.

My fear is that the late modern emphasis on creativity is serving as little more than a thin justification for the growing technological ability to extract and manipulate data, an act that is inherently destructive and violent. The underlying metaphysics of cybernetics attempts to instantiate a violent ontology, and the notion of humans as cocreators unwittingly underwrites this violence, as seen in its promotion of the cyborg to iconic status. As Hannah Arendt observed, violence can never beget genuine power and authority but only erode these necessary qualities for human flourishing.[19] Human beings can be powerful without necessarily resorting to violence, and they can also be violent because they are powerless. The gospel is an account of Christ's power and authority to create, redeem, and sustain creation and its creatures, but it is the result of the effortless spoken Word, and not violent physical effort. In short, the Word and the irenic words through which it is revealed need to be preserved, to resist the temptation of violently making icons into idols.

By way of illustrating what is at stake in resisting such idolatry, this chapter, as well as this book, concludes with a modest proposition: as IT, as well as other technologies that are transforming human beings and being human, becomes more ubiquitous and sophisticated, let the church in its worship preserve a privileged place for the Word in general, and the spoken word in particular. This is not to say that it should restrict worship to the sermon and spoken liturgy. Various technologies can be employed to frame occasions of oral proclamation and discourse, enabling their more effective transmission and efficacious reception. They are, however, a *frame* and not the centerpiece, for in the absence of the spoken word, they can inform and malform but not form; alone they can convey information, even knowledge, but not wisdom. Whenever the spoken word is displaced from the center, then worship easily degenerates into an entertainment commodity dispensed by a celebrity to be consumed by adoring customers. The rich imagery of the Eucharist is simply another meal if the words of institution are not spoken properly, and the most creative sermon is little more than a distracting amusement in the absence of an explicating word.

Words must be ordered to the truth of the Word which once uttered can never be captured. Consequently, they refuse to become objects or information that can be seized and manipulated. Rather, it is through words spoken in obedience to Jesus Christ that we are ushered into an eternal realm, and it is against the goodness, truth, and loveliness of this realm that we are measured and formed. It is in our acceptance of our lives as temporal, finite, and mortal creatures—and not through our frantic desire to create and be creative—that we disclose, that we become genuine icons of the image and likeness of *the* Creator and Redeemer. There is an old adage that a picture is worth a thousand words. Yet if the words an image inspires do not disclose what is good, true, and beautiful, then why waste the time to behold the image in the first place? Have our lives been even remotely enriched with the creation of hairy cacti, pig wings, and misshapen butterflies? This modest proposition serves to remind us that it is the God who creates and sustains us that has the first and final word: that our creaturely life is good, indeed very good. And most importantly, we encounter the God who redeems us in the Word made flesh, and not in our frantic desire—creative or otherwise—to extract and manipulate data from flesh.

Notes

Chapter 1

1. Aldous Huxley, *Brave New World* (New York: Harper and Row, 1946), 1.

2. George Grant, *Technology and Justice* (Notre Dame, IN: Notre Dame University Press, 1986), 11.

3. Ibid., 89.

4. George Grant, *Time as History* (Toronto: University of Toronto Press, 1995), 34.

5. Joan E. O'Donovan, *George Grant and the Twilight of Justice* (Toronto: University of Toronto Press, 1984), 119.

6. See his essay "The Question concerning Technology," in Martin Heidegger, *Basic Writings,* ed. David Farrell Krell (New York: HarperCollins, 1993), 307–42.

7. Huxley, *Brave New World*, 28.

8. See Paul Seabright, *The Company of Strangers: A Natural History of Economic Life* (Princeton, NJ: Princeton University Press, 2004), 13–28.

9. Ibid., 1.

10. See Richard Gray, "Mind Control," *Scotsman*, July 16, 2006. Accessed online.

11. Huxley, *Brave New World,* 161.

12. Ibid., 161–62.

13. As quoted in Grant, *Technology and Justice,* 9.

14. Beth Felker Jones, *Marks of His Wounds: Gender Politics and Bodily Resurrection* (Oxford: Oxford University Press, 2007), 12.

15. Cf. George Grant, 'The Computer Does Not Impose on Us the Ways It Should Be Used," in Abraham Rotstein, ed., *Beyond Industrial Growth* (Toronto: University of Toronto Press, 1976), 117–31.

16. See Book XIX/21.

17. I am indebted to David Hogue for this insight.

18. See H. Richard Niebuhr, *Radical Monotheism and Western Culture* (Louisville: Westminster/John Knox Press, 1993).

19. See Karl Barth, *Church Dogmatics* III/4 (Edinburgh: T&T Clark, 1961), 285–323.

20. See Matthew 22:37.

21. Ambrose, *On the Duties of the Clergy* 1.27/127.

22. See Matthew 22:34–40.

23. See Barth, *Church Dogmatics* III/4, 565–685.

24. Huxley, *Brave New World,* 163.

25. Grant, *Technology and Justice,* 32.

26. Ibid.

27. See Albert Borgmann, *Technology and the Character of Contemporary Life: A Philosophical Inquiry* (Chicago and London: University of Chicago Press, 1984), 40–48.

28. Grant, *Technology and Justice,* 32.

29. The following narrative is adapted from Brent Waters, *From Human to Posthuman: Christian Theology and Technology in a Postmodern World* (Aldershot, UK: Ashgate, 2006), 147–49.

30. Albert Borgmann, "Reply to My Critics," in Eric Higgs, Andrew Light, and David Strong, eds. *Technology and the Good Life?* (Chicago: University of Chicago Press, 2000), 356.

31. Albert Borgmann, *Power Failure: Christianity in the Culture of Technology* (Grand Rapids: Brazos Press, 2003), 22.

32. Borgmann, *Technology and the Character of Contemporary Life,* 204.

33. Ibid., 205.

34. See Borgmann, *Power Failure,* 117–28.

35. Ibid., 22.

36. See ibid., 125–28.

37. Grant, *Time as History,* 13.

Chapter 2

1. For a concise examination of these ethical issues, see Brent Waters, *Reproductive Technology: Towards a Theology of Procreative Stewardship* (Cleveland: Pilgrim Press, 2001).

2. See Genesis 30:1–2.

3. See Genesis 29:31–35, 30:1–22.

4. Rachel gives birth to a twelfth son, Benjamin, at a later date. See Genesis 35:16–26.

5. See, e.g., John A. Robertson, *Children of Choice: Freedom and the New Reproductive Technologies* (Princeton, NJ: Princeton University Press, 1994). For a theological critique, see Gilbert C. Meilaender, *Body, Soul, and Bioethics* (Notre Dame, IN: University of Notre Dame Press, 1995), 61–88.

6. Most proponents of reproductive freedom do not argue that individuals are entitled to have these options provided. Rather, access should not be restricted for those individuals with financial resources adequate to utilize them.

7. See Robertson, *Children of Choice*, 142–44.

8. See, e.g., Congregation for the Doctrine of Faith, *Instruction on Respect for Human Life in Its Origin and on the Dignity of Procreation: Replies to Certain Questions of the Day* (Vatican City: Vatican Polyglot Press, 1987).

9. See, e.g., Ted Peters, *For the Love of Children: Genetic Technology and the Future of the Family* (Louisville: Westminster/John Knox Press, 1996).

10. Ibid., 12.

11. See Ronald Cole-Turner and Brent Waters, *Pastoral Genetics: Theology and Care at the Beginning of Life* (Cleveland: Pilgrim Press, 1996).

12. Given this connotation, I will use the admittedly more awkward phrase "bodied creature" throughout the remainder of this article.

13. See 1 Corinthians 12.

14. See David Matzko McCarthy, *Sex and Love in the Home: A Theology of the Household* (London: SCM, 2001).

15. See Rodney Clapp, *Families at the Crossroads: Beyond Traditional and Modern Options* (Downers Grove, IL: InterVarsity Press, 1993), 149–69.

16. See Barbara Katz Rothman, *The Tentative Pregnancy: Amniocentesis and the Sexual Politics of Motherhood* (London: Pandora, 1994).

17. See Oliver O'Donovan, *Begotten or Made?* (Oxford: Clarendon Press, 1984).

18. See Waters, *Reproductive Technology*, 57–127.

19. See Peter Brown, *The Body and Society: Men, Women, and Sexual Renunciation in Early Christianity* (New York: Columbia University Press, 1988).

Chapter 3

1. See Paul Tillich, *Dynamics of Faith* (New York: Harper and Row, 1957), 1–29.

2. See H. Richard Niebuhr, *Radical Monotheism and Western Culture* (Louisville: Westminster/John Knox Press, 1993), 119.

3. See Bryan Appleyard, *Brave New Worlds: Genetics and Human Experience* (London: HarperCollins, 2000).

4. See, e.g., Aubrey de Grey, ed., "Strategies for Engineered Negligible Senescence: Why Genuine Control of Aging May Be Foreseeable," *Annals of the New York Academy of Science* 1019 (June 2004): 70–77; and "The War on Aging," in Im-

mortality Institute, *The Scientific Conquest of Death* (Buenos Aires: LibrosEnRed, 2004), 29–45.

5. "The Real Meaning of Genetics," *New Atlantis* 9 (summer 2005), 33.

6. See George Grant, *Technology and Justice* (Notre Dame, IN: University of Notre Dame Press, 1986), 32.

7. See Stanley Hauerwas, *Suffering Presence: Theological Reflections on Medicine, the Mentally Handicapped, and the Church* (Notre Dame, IN: University of Notre Dame Press, 1986), 23–83.

8. See Augustine, *A Treatise on the Merits and Forgiveness of Sins, and on the Baptism of Infants,* Book I.

9. See John Passmore, *The Perfectibility of Man* (New York: Charles Scribner's Sons, 1970).

10. See Augustine, *City of God* XIII.

11. See John Swinton and Brian Brock, eds., *Theology, Disability, and the New Genetics: Why Science Needs the Church* (London: T&T Clark, 2007).

12. See Psalms 8:3–8.

13. See Francis Fukuyama, *Our Posthuman Future: Consequences of the Biotechnology Revolution* (New York: Farrar, Straus and Giroux, 2002).

14. See Hannah Arendt, *The Human Condition* (Chicago: University of Chicago Press, 1980), 7–11.

15. See Jürgen Habermas, *The Future of Human Nature* (Cambridge, UK: Polity, 2003).

16. See Oliver O'Donovan, *Begotten or Made?* (Oxford: Clarendon Press, 1984).

Chapter 4

1. As quoted in George Grant, *Technology and Justice* (Notre Dame, IN: University of Notre Dame Press, 1986), 9. Grant had entered this proverb earlier (1942) in his personal journal. See Arthur Davis and Peter C. Emberley, eds. *The Collected Works of George Grant,* vol. 1, *1933–1950* (Toronto: University of Toronto Press, 2000), 17.

2. See Karl Barth, *Church Dogmatics* III/4 (Edinburgh: T&T Clark), 285–323.

3. See, e.g., Stephen Clark, *Biology and Christian Ethics* (Cambridge: Cambridge University Press, 2000).

4. See, e.g., Hannah Arendt, *The Human Condition* (Chicago: University of Chicago Press, 1998), 7–21; and Hans Jonas, *The Imperative of Responsibility: In Search of an Ethics for the Technological Age* (Chicago: University of Chicago Press, 1984), 1–24.

5. See chapter 5.

Chapter 5

1. For a concise overview of recent and anticipated developments in regenerative medicine, see William A. Haseltine, "Regenerative Medicine: A Future Healing Art," *Brookings Review* 21, no. 1 (winter 2003), 38–43.

2. See Stephen S. Hall, *Merchants of Immortality: Chasing the Dream of Human Life Extension* (Boston: Houghton Mifflin, 2003).

3. This shift has already occurred to a significant extent. See H. Tristram Engelhardt Jr., *The Foundations of Bioethics* (New York: Oxford University Press, 1996); Leon R. Kass, *Toward a More Natural Science: Biology and Human Affairs* (New York: Free Press, 1985), 157–246; Gerald P. McKenny, *To Relieve the Human Condition: Bioethics, Technology, and the Body* (Albany: SUNY Press, 1997); and Paul Ramsey, *The Patient as Person: Explorations in Medical Ethics* (New Haven: Yale University Press, 1970), 113–64.

4. A normal human cell can divide a limited number of times (usually around fifty-two) until it reaches its senescence phase, when it can no longer divide.

5. See, e.g., Donna J. Haraway, *Simians, Cyborgs, and Women: The Reinvention of Nature* (London: Free Association Books, 1991), 149–81; and Philip Hefner, *Technology and Human Becoming* (Minneapolis: Fortress, 2003), 73–88; cf. Elaine L. Graham, *Representations of the Post/Human: Monsters, Aliens and Others in Popular Culture* (Manchester, UK: Manchester University Press, 2002), 200–220.

6. For an overview of this ambitious agenda, see the Web sites of the World Transhumanist Association, http://www.transhumanism.org/index.htm.

7. See "The Road to Posthumanity," http://www.aleph.se/Trans/Intro/path .html.

8. See Ray Kurzweil, *The Age of Spiritual Machines: When Computers Exceed Human Intelligence* (New York: Penguin Books, 2000), 118–29; and Hans Moravec, *Mind Children: The Future of Robot and Human Intelligence* (Cambridge: Harvard University Press, 1988), 100–124.

9. Nick Bostrom, "Transhumanist Values," http://www.nickbostrom.com/ ethics/values.html.

10. Ibid.

11. See Hans Moravec, *Robot: Mere Machines to Transcendent Mind* (Oxford: Oxford University Press, 1999), 191–211.

12. See N. Katherine Hayles, *How We Became Posthuman: Virtual Bodies in Cybernetics, Literature, and Informatics* (Chicago: University of Chicago Press, 1999), 279–82.

13. See ibid., 286–87.

14. Ibid., 5.

15. Ibid., 291.

16. See Francis Fukuyama, *Our Posthuman Future: Consequences of the Biotechnology Revolution* (New York: Farrar, Straus and Giroux, 2002), 14.

17. Ibid., 130.

18. See ibid., 140–43.

19. Ibid., 173.

20. See ibid., 7–8.

21. Ibid., 10 (emphasis original).

22. See ibid., 181–218.

23. Leon Kass, *Life, Liberty and the Defense of Dignity: The Challenge for Bioethics* (San Francisco: Encounter Books, 2002), 6.

24. See Leon R. Kass, *Toward a More Natural Science: Biology and Human Affairs* (New York: Free Press, 1985), 299–317.

25. Kass, *Life, Liberty and the Defense of Dignity,* 20.

26. See ibid., 17–19.

27. See Kass, *Toward a More Natural Science,* 25–40.

28. See Kass, *Life, Liberty and the Defense of Dignity,* 8–12.

29. Kass, *Toward a More Natural Science,* 71.

30. George Grant, *Lament for a Nation: The Defeat of Canadian Nationalism* (Montreal: McGill-Queen's University Press, 2000), 100.

31. Ibid.

32. Eric O. Springsted, ed., *Simone Weil* (Maryknoll, NY: Orbis Books, 1998), 73.

33. Ibid.

34. See Arthur Davis, ed., *Collected Works of George Grant,* vol. 2, *1951–1959* (Toronto: University of Toronto Press, 2002), 483–89.

35. See Harris Athanasiadis, *George Grant and the Theology of the Cross: The Christian Foundations of His Thought* (Toronto: University of Toronto Press, 2001).

36. See Kass, *Life, Liberty and the Defense of Dignity,* 96–102.

37. See ibid., 69–72.

38. See McKenny, *To Relieve the Human Condition,* 143–46.

39. See George Grant, *Technology and Justice* (Notre Dame, IN: Notre Dame University Press, 1986), 11–34.

40. George Grant, *Time as History* (Toronto: University of Toronto Press, 1995), 45–46.

Chapter 6

1. See, e.g., Brent Waters and Ronald R. Cole-Turner, eds., *God and the Embryo: Religious Voices on Stem Cells and Cloning* (Washington, DC: Georgetown University Press, 2003).

2. See, e.g., President's Council on Bioethics, *Beyond Therapy: Biotechnology and the Pursuit of Happiness* (Washington, DC: President's Council on Bioethics, 2003).

3. See chapter 5.

4. See, e.g., Stanley Hauerwas, *Suffering Presence: Theological Reflections on Medicine, the Mentally Handicapped, and the Church* (Notre Dame: University of Notre Dame Press, 1986).

5. See John A. Robertson, *Children of Choice: Freedom and the New Reproductive Technologies* (Princeton, NJ: Princeton University Press, 1994).

6. See Hannah Arendt, *The Human Condition* (Chicago: University of Chicago Press, 1998).

7. See, e.g., Leon Kass, *Toward a More Natural Science: Biology and Human Affairs* (New York: Free Press, 1985), 299–317; and *Life, Liberty and the Defense of Dignity: The Challenge for Bioethics* (San Francisco: Encounter Books, 2002), 257–74.

8. See Elaine L. Graham, *Representations of the Post/Human: Monsters, Aliens and Others in Popular Culture* (New Brunswick, NJ: Rutgers University Press, 2002), 176–220; N. Katherine Hayles, *How We Became Posthuman: Virtual Bodies in Cybernetics, Literature, and Informatics* (Chicago: University of Chicago Press, 1999); and Brent Waters, *From Human to Posthuman: Christian Theology and Technology in a Postmodern World* (Aldershot, UK, and Burlington: Ashgate, 2006), 1–93.

9. See George Grant, *Time as History* (Toronto: University of Toronto Press, 1995).

10. Eric O. Springsted, *Simone Weil* (Maryknoll, New York: Orbis Books, 1998), 73.

11. See, e.g., George Grant, *Technology and Empire: Perspectives on North America* (Toronto: Anansi, 1969), 15–40.

12. See, e.g., Gordon D. Kaufman, *In the Beginning . . . Creativity* (Minneapolis: Fortress, 2004).

13. See, e.g., Kass, *Toward a More Natural Science,* and *Life, Liberty and the Defense of Dignity;* and Francis Fukuyama, *Our Posthuman Future: Consequences of the Biotechnology Revolution* (New York: Farrar, Straus and Giroux, 2002).

14. See Ronald R. Cole-Turner and Brent Waters, *Pastoral Genetics: Theology and Care at the Beginning of Life* (Cleveland: Pilgrim Press, 1996), 93–110.

15. See Oliver O'Donovan, *Resurrection and Moral Order: An Outline for Evangelical Ethics* (Grand Rapids: Eerdmans, 1986).

16. Ibid., 14.

17. See ibid., 16–21.

18. Ibid., 17 (emphasis original).

19. See ibid., 22–27.

20. Ibid., 22.

21. Ibid., 23.

Chapter 7

1. For an overview, see Stephen S. Hall, *Merchants of Immortality: Chasing the Dream of Human Life Extension* (Boston: Houghton Mifflin, 2003).

2. See Immortality Institute, *The Scientific Conquest of Death: Essays on Infinite Lifespans* (Buenos Aires: LibrosEnRed, 2004).

3. See Leon R. Kass, *Toward a More Natural Science: Biology and Human Affairs* (New York: Free Press, 1985), 299–317, and *Life, Liberty and the Defense of Dignity: The Challenge for Bioethics* (San Francisco: Encounter Books, 2002), 257–74.

4. See Hannah Arendt, *The Human Condition* (Chicago: University of Chicago Press, 1998), 8–9.

5. See ibid., 97.

6. Ibid., 246.

7. See ibid., 96–97.

8. See ibid., 19–20.

9. See Charles Norris Cochrane, *Christianity and Classical Culture: A Study of Thought and Action from Augustus to Augustine* (Indianapolis: Amagi Books, 2003).

10. See George Grant, *Time as History* (Toronto: University of Toronto Press, 1995).

11. See chapter 1.

12. See, e.g., George Grant's essay "Thinking about Technology," in *Technology and Justice* (Notre Dame, IN: University of Notre Dame Press, 1986).

13. See *Human Condition*, 84–85.

14. Ibid., 18.

15. Ibid., 50.

16. See ibid., 221.

17. See ibid., 10–11.

18. See 1 Corinthians 15:26.

19. See John 1:1–4; see also Philippians 2:5–11.

20. See St. Augustine, *City of God* XXII/30.

21. See St. Augustine, *Confessions* I/1.

22. See St. Augustine, *City of God* XIV.

23. See Karl Barth, *Church Dogmatics* III/4 §55.

24. See Gilbert Meilaender, *Bioethics: A Primer for Christians* (Grand Rapids: Eerdmans, 1996), 24–25.

25. See John F. Kilner, *Life on the Line: Ethics, Aging, Ending Patients' Lives, and Allocating Vital Resources* (Grand Rapids: Eerdmans, 1992), 65–69.

26. See Brent Waters, "Welcoming Children into our Homes: A Theological Reflection on Adoption," *Scottish Journal of Theology* 55, no. 4 (2002), 424–37.

27. See David C. Thomasma and Glenn C. Graeber, *Euthanasia: Toward an Ethical Social Policy* (New York: Continuum, 1991), 85–86.

28. See Barth, *Church Dogmatics* III/4, 400–409.

29. See Paul Ramsey, *The Patient as Person: Explorations in Medical Ethics* (New Haven: Yale University Press, 1970), 134.

30. 1 Corinthians 15:55.

Chapter 8

1. See, e.g., Francis Fukuyama, *Our Posthuman Future: Consequences of the Biotechnology Revolution* (New York: Farrar, Straus and Giroux, 2002).

2. See, e.g., Philip Hefner, *Technology and Human Becoming* (Minneapolis: Fortress Press, 2003).

3. See, e.g., Ray Kurzweil, *The Age of Spiritual Machines: When Computers Exceed Human Intelligence* (New York: Penguin Books, 2000), and *The Singularity Is Near: When Humans Transcend Biology* (London: Penguin Books, 2005); see also Hans Moravec, *Mind Children: The Future of Robot and Human Intelligence* (Cambridge: Harvard University Press, 1988), and *Robot: Mere Machines to Transcendent Mind* (Oxford: Oxford University Press, 1999).

4. I examine the emergence of a posthuman world in much greater detail in my book, *From Human to Posthuman: Christian Theology and Technology in a Postmodern World* (Aldershot, UK, and Burlington: Ashgate, 2006).

5. See Martin Heidegger, *The Question concerning Technology and Other Essays* (New York: Harper and Row, 1977); see also Michael E. Zimmerman, *Heidegger's Confrontation with Modernity: Technology, Politics, Art* (Bloomington: Indiana University Press, 1990).

6. N. Katherine Hayles, *How We Became Posthuman: Virtual Bodies in Cybernetics, Literature, and Informatics* (Chicago: University of Chicago Press, 1999), 7.

7. See "Meeting Transcript," January 17, 2002, http://www.bioethics.gov/transcripts/jan02/jan17full.html#2.

8. Emphasis added.

9. See John Passmore, *The Perfectibility of Man* (New York: Charles Scribner's Sons, 1970).

10. See Paul Ramsey, *Fabricated Man: The Ethics of Genetic Control* (New Haven: Yale University Press, 1970), 151–52.

11. See ibid., 87–88.

12. See 1 Corinthians 15:26.

13. For a more detailed explication, see Waters, *From Human to Posthuman*, 95–150.

14. See Revelation 1:8.

15. See John 1:14.

16. See Philippians 2:6–8.

17. See Oliver O'Donovan, *Resurrection and Moral Order: An Outline for Evangelical Ethics* (Grand Rapids: Eerdmans, 1986).

18. Ibid., 14.

19. See ibid., 16–21.

20. See Robert Spaemann, *Persons: The Difference between "Someone" and "Something"* (Oxford: Oxford University Press, 2006), 78–80.

21. See O'Donovan, *Resurrection and Moral Order,* 22–27.

22. See George Grant, *Technology and Justice* (Notre Dame, IN: Notre Dame University Press, 1986), 11–34.

23. See ibid., 19–21.

24. Ibid., 32.

Chapter 9

1. http://www.newscientist.com/article/mg18124365.400-art-but-not-as-we-know-it.html. See also "Art, but Not as We Know It," *New Scientist* 181, no. 2436 (February 28, 2004), 44–46.

2. See, e.g., Hannah Arendt, *The Life of the Mind,* vol. 1, *Thinking* (San Diego: Harcourt, 1978), 69–78.

3. See Celia E. Deane-Drummond, *Creation through Wisdom: Theology and the New Biology* (Edinburgh: T&T Clark, 2000).

4. As quoted in Warren Bryan Martin, *A College of Character: Renewing the Purpose and Content of College Education* (San Francisco: Jossey-Bass, 1982), 13.

5. See Jacques Ellul, *The Humiliation of the Word* (Grand Rapids: Eerdmans, 1985), 71–106.

6. See Michael Heim, *The Metaphysics of Virtual Reality* (New York: Oxford University Press, 1993), 41–54.

7. See Philip Hefner, *Theology and Human Becoming* (Minneapolis: Fortress, 2003), 73–88.

8. See Donna J. Haraway, *Simians, Cyborgs, and Women: The Reinvention of Women* (New York: Routledge, 1991), 149–82.

9. See Eric O. Springsted, ed., *Simone Weil* (Maryknoll, NY: Orbis, 1998), 73.

10. See, e.g., Philip Hefner, *The Human Factor: Evolution, Culture, and Religion* (Minneapolis: Fortress, 1993); and A. R. Peacocke, *Creation and the World of Science: The Bampton Lectures, 1978* (Oxford: Clarendon Press, 1979).

11. See Hans Moravec, *Mind Children: The Future of Robot and Human Intelligence* (Cambridge: Harvard University Press, 1988), and *Robot: Mere Machines to Transcendent Mind* (Oxford: Oxford University Press, 1999).

12. See Ray Kurzweil, *The Age of Spiritual Machines: When Computers Exceed Human Intelligence* (New York: Penguin Books, 2000), and *The Singularity Is Near: When Humans Transcend Biology* (New York: Penguin Books, 2005).

13. See Pierre Teilhard de Chardin, *The Future of Man* (London: Collins, 1964).

14. See Springsted, ed., *Simone Weil,* 78.

15. See George Grant, *Lament for a Nation: The Defeat of Canadian Nationalism* (Montreal: McGill-Queen's University Press, 2000), 99–100; and Arthur Davis, ed., *Collected Works of George Grant,* vol. 2, *1951–1959* (Toronto: University of Toronto Press, 2002), 483–89.

16. See Ellul, *Humiliation of the Word,* 71–102.

17. See Ernan McMullin, "Cosmic Purpose and the Contingency of Human Evolution," *Theology Today 55,* no. 3 (1998), 389–414.

18. See Oliver O'Donovan, *Resurrection and Moral Order* (Grand Rapids: Eerdmans, 1986).

19. See Hannah Arendt, *On Violence* (New York: Harcourt, Brace and World, 1970).

Bibliography

Ambrose. *On the Duties of the Clergy,* in *Select Works and Letters.* Vol. 10 of *Select Library of the Nicene and Post-Nicene Fathers of the Christian Church,* ser. 2, edited by Philip Schaff and Henry Wace. Edinburgh: T&T Clark, 1989.

Appleyard, Bryan. *Brave New Worlds: Genetics and Human Experience.* London: HarperCollins, 2000.

Arendt, Hannah. *The Human Condition.* Chicago: University of Chicago Press, 1980.

————. *The Life of the Mind.* Vol. 1, *Thinking* San Diego: Harcourt, 1978.

————. *On Violence* New York: Harcourt, Brace and World, 1970.

"Art, but Not as We Know It," *New Scientist* 181:2436 (February 28, 2004): 44–46.

Athanasiadis, Harris. *George Grant and the Theology of the Cross: The Christian Foundations of His Thought.* Toronto: University of Toronto Press, 2001.

Augustine. *Concerning the City of God against the Pagans.* New York: Penguin Books, 1984.

————. *The Confessions.* Garden City, NJ: Image Books, 1960.

————. *A Treatise on the Merits and Forgiveness of Sins, and on the Baptism of Infants.* Vol. 5 of *Select Library of the Nicene and Post-Nicene Fathers of the Christian Church,* ser. 1, edited by Philip Schaff, Edinburgh: T&T Clark, 1991.

Barth, Karl. *Church Dogmatics* III/4. Edinburgh: T&T Clark, 1961.

Borgmann, Albert. *Power Failure: Christianity in the Culture of Technology.* Grand Rapids: Brazos Press, 2003.

———. *Technology and the Character of Contemporary Life: A Philosophical Inquiry.* Chicago: University of Chicago Press, 1984.

Bostrom, Nick. "Transhumanist Values," http://www.nickbostrom.com/ethics/values.html.

Brown, Peter. *The Body and Society: Men, Women, and Sexual Renunciation in Early Christianity.* New York: Columbia University Press, 1988.

Clapp, Rodney. *Families at the Crossroads: Beyond Traditional and Modern Options.* Downers Grove, IL: InterVarsity Press, 1993.

Clark, Stephen. *Biology and Christian Ethics.* Cambridge: Cambridge University Press, 2000.

Cochrane, Charles Norris. *Christianity and Classical Culture: A Study of Thought and Action from Augustus to Augustine.* Indianapolis: Amagi Books, 2003.

Cohen, Eric. "The Real Meaning of Genetics," *New Atlantis* 9 (summer 2005): 29–41.

Cole-Turner, Ronald, and Brent Waters. *Pastoral Genetics: Theology and Care at the Beginning of Life.* Cleveland: Pilgrim Press, 1996.

Congregation for the Doctrine of Faith, *Instruction on Respect for Human Life in Its Origin and on the Dignity of Procreation: Replies to Certain Questions of the Day.* Vatican City: Vatican Polyglot Press, 1987.

Davis, Arthur, ed. *Collected Works of George Grant.* Vol. 2, *1951–1959.* Toronto: University of Toronto Press, 2002.

Davis, Arthur, and Peter C. Emberley, eds. *The Collected Works of George Grant.* Vol. 1, *1933–1950.* Toronto: University of Toronto Press, 2000.

Deane-Drummond, Celia E. *Creation through Wisdom: Theology and the New Biology.* Edinburgh: T&T Clark, 2000.

de Grey, Aubrey, ed. "Strategies for Engineered Negligible Senescence: Why Genuine Control of Aging May Be Foreseeable," *Annals of the New York Academy of Science* 1019 (June 2004).

Ellul, Jacques. *The Humiliation of the Word.* Grand Rapids: Eerdmans, 1985.

Engelhardt, H. Tristram Jr. *The Foundations of Bioethics.* New York: Oxford University Press, 1996.

Fukuyama, Francis. *Our Posthuman Future: Consequences of the Biotechnology Revolution.* New York: Farrar, Straus and Giroux, 2002.

Graham, Elaine L. *Representations of the Post/Human: Monsters, Aliens and Others in Popular Culture*. Manchester, UK: Manchester University Press, 2002.

Grant, George. *Lament for a Nation: The Defeat of Canadian Nationalism*. Montreal: McGill-Queen's University Press, 2000.

———. *Technology and Empire: Perspectives on North America*. Toronto: Anansi, 1969.

———. *Technology and Justice*. Notre Dame, IN: Notre Dame University Press, 1986.

———. *Time as History*. Toronto: University of Toronto Press, 1995.

Gray, Richard. "Mind Control," *Scotsman*, July 16, 2006. Accessed online.

Habermas, Jürgen. *The Future of Human Nature*. Cambridge, UK: Polity, 2003.

Hall, Stephen S. *Merchants of Immortality: Chasing the Dream of Human Life Extension*. Boston: Houghton Mifflin, 2003.

Haraway, Donna J. *Simians, Cyborgs, and Women: The Reinvention of Nature*. London: Free Association Books, 1991.

Haseltine, William A. "Regenerative Medicine: A Future Healing Art," *Brookings Review* 21, no. 1 (winter 2003).

Hauerwas, Stanley. *Suffering Presence: Theological Reflections on Medicine, the Mentally Handicapped, and the Church*. Notre Dame, IN: University of Notre Dame Press, 1986.

Hayles, N. Katherine. *How We Became Posthuman: Virtual Bodies in Cybernetics, Literature, and Informatics*. Chicago: University of Chicago Press, 1999.

Hefner, Philip. *The Human Factor: Evolution, Culture, and Religion*. Minneapolis: Fortress, 1993.

———. *Technology and Human Becoming*. Minneapolis: Fortress, 2003.

Heidegger, Martin. *The Question concerning Technology and Other Essays*. New York: Harper and Row, 1977.

Heim, Michael. *The Metaphysics of Virtual Reality*. New York: Oxford University Press, 1993.

Huxley, Aldous. *Brave New World*. New York: Harper and Row, 1946.

Immortality Institute. *The Scientific Conquest of Death*. Buenos Aires: LibrosEnRed, 2004.

Jonas, Hans. *The Imperative of Responsibility: In Search of an Ethics for the Technological Age*. Chicago: University of Chicago Press, 1984.

Jones, Beth Felker. *Marks of His Wounds: Gender Politics and Bodily Resurrection*. Oxford: Oxford University Press, 2007.

Kass, Leon. *Life, Liberty and the Defense of Dignity: The Challenge for Bioethics*. San Francisco: Encounter Books, 2002.

―――. *Toward a More Natural Science: Biology and Human Affairs*. New York: Free Press, 1985.

Kaufman, Gordon D. *In the Beginning . . . Creativity*. Minneapolis: Fortress Press, 2004.

Kilner, John F. *Life on the Line: Ethics, Aging. Ending Patients' Lives, and Allocating Vital Resources*. Grand Rapids: Eerdmans, 1992.

Kurzweil, Ray. *The Age of Spiritual Machines: When Computers Exceed Human Intelligence*. New York: Penguin Books, 2000.

―――. *The Singularity Is Near: When Humans Transcend Biology*. New York: Penguin Books, 2005.

Light, Andrew, and David Strong, eds. *Technology and the Good Life?* Chicago: University of Chicago Press, 2000.

Martin, Warren Bryan. *A College of Character: Renewing the Purpose and Content of College Education*. San Francisco: Jossey-Bass, 1982.

McCarthy, David Matzko. *Sex and Love in the Home: A Theology of the Household*. London: SCM, 2001.

McKenny, Gerald P. *To Relieve the Human Condition: Bioethics, Technology, and the Body*. Albany: SUNY Press, 1997.

McMullin, Ernan. "Cosmic Purpose and the Contingency of Human Evolution," *Theology Today* 55:3 (1998): 389–414.

Meilaender, Gilbert. *Bioethics: A Primer for Christians*. Grand Rapids: Eerdmans, 1996.

―――. *Body, Soul, and Bioethics*. Notre Dame, IN: University of Notre Dame Press, 1995.

Moravec, Hans. *Mind Children: The Future of Robot and Human Intelligence*. Cambridge: Harvard University Press, 1988.

―――. *Robot: Mere Machines to Transcendent Mind*. Oxford: Oxford University Press, 1999.

Niebuhr, H. Richard. *Radical Monotheism and Western Culture*. Louisville: Westminster/John Knox Press, 1993.

O'Donovan, Joan E. *George Grant and the Twilight of Justice*. Toronto: University of Toronto Press, 1984.

O'Donovan, Oliver. *Begotten or Made?* Oxford: Clarendon Press, 1984.

———. *Resurrection and Moral Order: An Outline for Evangelical Ethics*. Grand Rapids: Eerdmans, 1986.

Passmore, John. *The Perfectibility of Man*. New York: Charles Scribner's Sons, 1970.

Peacocke, A. R. *Creation and the World of Science: The Bampton Lectures, 1978*. Oxford: Clarendon Press, 1979.

Peters, Ted. *For the Love of Children: Genetic Technology and the Future of the Family*. Louisville: Westminster/John Knox Press, 1996.

President's Council on Bioethics. *Beyond Therapy: Biotechnology and the Pursuit of Happiness*. Washington, DC: President's Council on Bioethics, 2003.

Ramsey, Paul. *Fabricated Man: The Ethics of Genetic Control*. New Haven: Yale University Press, 1970.

———. *The Patient as Person: Explorations in Medical Ethics*. New Haven: Yale University Press, 1970.

Robertson, John A. *Children of Choice: Freedom and the New Reproductive Technologies*. Princeton, NJ: Princeton University Press, 1994.

Rothman, Barbara Katz. *The Tentative Pregnancy: Amniocentesis and the Sexual Politics of Motherhood*. London: Pandora, 1994.

Rotstein, Abraham, ed. *Beyond Industrial Growth*. Toronto: University of Toronto Press, 1976.

Seabright, Paul. *The Company of Strangers: A Natural History of Economic Life*. Princeton, NJ: Princeton University Press, 2004.

Spaemann, Robert. *Persons: The Difference between "Someone" and "Something."* Oxford: Oxford University Press, 2006.

Springsted, Eric O., ed. *Simone Weil*. Maryknoll, NY: Orbis Books, 1998.

Swinton, John, and Brian Brock, eds. *Theology, Disability, and the New Genetics: Why Science Needs the Church*. London: T&T Clark, 2007.

Teilhard de Chardin, Pierre. *The Future of Man*. London: Collins, 1964.

Thomasma, David C., and Glenn C. Graeber, *Euthanasia: Toward an Ethical Social Policy*. New York: Continuum, 1991.

Tillich, Paul. *Dynamics of Faith*. New York: Harper and Row, 1957.

Waters, Brent. *From Human to Posthuman: Christian Theology and Technology in a Postmodern World*. Aldershot, UK: Ashgate, 2006.

———. *Reproductive Technology: Towards a Theology of Procreative Stewardship*. Cleveland: Pilgrim Press, 2001.

———. "Welcoming Children into Our Homes: A Theological Reflection on Adoption," *Scottish Journal of Theology* 55, no. 4 (2002): 424–37.

Waters, Brent, and Ronald R. Cole-Turner, eds. *God and the Embryo: Religious Voices on Stem Cells and Cloning.* Washington, DC: Georgetown University Press, 2003.

Zimmerman, Michael E. *Heidegger's Confrontation with Modernity: Technology, Politics, Art.* Bloomington: Indiana University Press, 1990.

Index